POST-TRAUMATIC STRESS DISORDER

The Essential Guide

Glenys
O'Connell

Post-Traumatic Stress Disorder – The Essential Guide is also available in accessible formats for people with any degree of visual impairment. The large print edition and eBook (with accessibility features enabled) are available from Need2Know. Please let us know if there are any special features you require and we will do our best to accommodate your needs.

First published in Great Britain in 2011 by
Need2Know
Remus House
Coltsfoot Drive
Peterborough
PE2 9BF
Telephone 01733 898103
Fax 01733 313524
www.need2knowbooks.co.uk

Contents

Introduction

Post-traumatic stress disorder (PTSD) has been in the news a lot recently, usually to do with its effects on soldiers involved in battlefield situations.

You may have heard some of the symptoms described and thought: 'Gee, that sounds like me . . . but I've not been in a war.' Well, even if you've not experienced battle conditions, you may still have PTSD. Frequently referred to as 'the normal reaction of a normal person to an abnormal event', PTSD can affect anyone who has been caught up in a terrifying incident, from a serious car accident to a natural disaster, from child abuse to war, from a mugging or a rape to any other kind of crime where you might think your life is in danger.

PTSD can affect anyone who has experienced a traumatic experience, particularly where their own or someone else's life is threatened:

Elise suffered only mild injuries in a traffic accident and was able to comfort her badly injured friend until the paramedics arrived.

Jack, a decorated military officer, considered himself battle-hardened after several tours of duty in war-torn countries.

Dani left an abusive childhood behind when she went to university; achieved a PhD and got a top job in one of the 'caring professions'.

Ali, an experienced rescue worker, toiled round the clock to pull survivors out of the rubble of their homes following an earthquake.

Izzy always followed the construction site safety rules; so he was shocked when an accident left him permanently disabled.

Anna was the victim of a violent rape. From being a bright, gregarious young woman, she became withdrawn, introverted, chronically anxious and sometimes suicidal.

Six different people (not real names) with different stories, yet they all have one thing in common. All experienced an alarming onset of symptoms, including flashbacks, panic attacks, angry outbursts, and difficulty sleeping. And all were diagnosed with post-traumatic stress disorder.

While it's normal to feel shocked and upset following a traumatic event, PTSD can ambush its victims days, weeks, months – or in some cases, years – after the event. It can be terrifying. 'I actually thought I was losing my mind,' is a common refrain heard from PTSD patients.

Many people with PTSD symptoms, including those in the military, police, fire and rescue services, are reluctant to seek treatment because they fear it will affect their careers with the taint of mental health problems or even cowardice. Tragically, such repression and lack of treatment can lead to relationship and family break-ups, dysfunctional behaviour, loss of employment, self-destructive behaviour or even violence towards others.

Many PTSD survivors report that they have had difficulties in getting a correct diagnosis and treatment. With the scheduled return of thousands of soldiers and other military personnel who have experienced severe trauma in combat, it is vital that these issues are addressed. The way we go about the diagnosis, treatment, care and understanding of PTSD sufferers will have far-reaching effects on many aspects of our society.

In recent years, medical and mental health professionals have accepted that any event stressful enough to have a traumatic effect on the people involved – from loss of a loved one to a serious car accident or witnessing a frightening assault – can be sufficient to trigger symptoms of PTSD. Any situation in which a person fears for their safety, or that of another person, can trigger PTSD.

Now, the good news – PTSD is curable. The bad news is that it may take quite a long time, possibly even years, before you feel safe in your own skin again if you've experienced a traumatic event that has left you with PTSD symptoms.

There is help available to treat and cure this frightening condition so that sufferers can get their lives back to normal. But it's a complex illness with many variations and there is no 'quick fix' cure. The route towards feeling better is to get professional help.

You are taking that first step for yourself or someone you care about by reading this book. Understanding that there is a problem and a solution is the first step. The next is to seek treatment, help and support. There are effective treatments today to help a person experiencing PTSD to return to a normal life. While the information in this book should not be taken as medical advice, we hope that it will prompt you to take that next step and get the professional help and treatment that will give you back control over your life.

Disclaimer

This book is only for general information about post-traumatic stress disorder and is not intended to replace medical advice, although it can be used alongside it. Anyone who suspects they may have post-traumatic stress disorder should contact their GP in the first instance.

Chapter One

What is Post-Traumatic Stress Disorder?

We'll look at PTSD in more detail later in the book, but here's a brief explanation:

Post-traumatic stress disorder, sometimes called post-traumatic stress syndrome, is an anxiety disorder which usually appears after a very distressing traumatic event, although sometimes it is connected to long-term stress such as domestic abuse, child abuse, or bullying at work or at school.

What causes PTSD?

People who experience severe stress, either in one frightening traumatic event or in a series of ongoing highly stressful conditions, may develop this condition. It's not unusual to have an acute stress disorder after something awful has happened, and this usually begins to fade as you settle back into your life and feel safe again. However, if the feelings following the stressful or frightening event continue for more than a month, it's quite likely you have PTSD and need help in getting back to normal.

Could I have PTSD?

If you have experienced a frightening event, such as a serious car accident, natural disaster, rape, physical assault, or battle conditions, and are now experiencing symptoms such as nightmares or flashbacks, a feeling of emotional numbness, anxiety, disengagement with the world around you, a sense of being in danger and restless, (see later chapters for a fuller listing of PTSD symptoms) then you probably should discuss PTSD with your doctor.

A short history of PTSD

Like a number of other mental health conditions, Post-traumatic stress disorder has been around a long time but only relatively recently have the collective symptoms been recognised as a disorder in their own right. While PTSD can affect anyone, it has been brought to the forefront today by the sufferings of soldiers traumatised in combat. It's expected that growing numbers of men and women returning from war zones such as Afghanistan and Iraq will be in need of help to cope with PTSD.

While PTSD has long been related to the military – the earliest observations of stress effects on soldiers in combat were recorded when the Trojans fought the Greeks in 1200 BC – it hasn't always been understood. In what could be seen as a terrible stain on history, about 306 British and Commonwealth soldiers were branded cowards and executed by firing squads during WW1 – men who were more than likely suffering from the mental and emotional dysfunction that we now call PTSD. Their families were left to cope not only with the grief of losing a loved one, but with the shame of that person's 'cowardice'. It's worth noting that, according to the records, only 25 soldiers in the German army were executed for 'cowardice' and no American soldiers were executed for similar reasons.

But you don't have to be in a battle situation to experience PTSD.

Historically there are many references to symptoms we now recognise as post-traumatic stress caused by frightening events. Egyptian doctors wrote about 'hysteria' occurring in those who had undergone dangerous or life-threatening experiences as early as 2000 BC. The Greek philosopher and writer, Homer, in his Odyssey, spoke of symptoms that we would now recognise as flashbacks and 'survivor's guilt' in 800 BC. The earliest recorded incidence of a soldier with PTSD symptoms was in the Greco-Trojan War of around 1200 BC. At that time an observer noted that a soldier who had seen a friend fighting alongside him killed had become blind – without any apparent physical reason – and never regained his sight. Was this the mind's way of protecting this man from seeing any further terrible and traumatic sights?

PTSD usually develops in people who have been exposed to terrifying, life-threatening situations, which is why the symptoms have long been associated with the military in war. Before it became recognised as a diagnosable emotional condition, it was referred to variously as 'battle fatigue', 'gross stress reaction', 'combat fatigue' or 'shell shock'. Soldiers suffering these symptoms after the American Civil War were described as having 'soldier's heart'.

Despite recognition of a connection between trauma and the collection of symptoms we now call PTSD, it has for many years been ignored or dismissed. People presenting with PTSD symptoms were either treated for other mental health conditions, or worse, accused of malingering and told to 'get over it'.

It wasn't until American veterans of the Vietnam War in the late 1960s and early 1970s pushed the authorities to accept the fact that many were suffering from serious and long-lasting emotional and mental problems as a result of their war experiences, that PTSD began to be an accepted diagnosis. At that time doctors were calling it Post-Vietnam Syndrome although, of course, the symptoms weren't confined to those who had served in Vietnam.

Current day viewpoints:

Studies from respected institutions such as King's College, London, suggest that as many as one in four UK soldiers returning from Afghanistan and Iraq are trying to cope with mental or emotional problems caused by their experiences. Some estimate that 17,000 members of the armed forces are suffering from anxiety and depression, with as many as 3,500 members of the reserves also facing these difficulties. It seems obvious that necessary support and treatment must be provided for these men and women to prevent them suffering further with financial difficulties, family and marital strife, the loss of homes, difficulties with jobs, and inadequate treatment for both physical and mental wounds brought about by the dysfunction of PTSD.

The inadequacy of treatment is apparent in the wide discrepancies between Ministry of Defence statistics and figures reported by veterans' groups and some respected academic studies. The MoD reports indicate that in the three year period from 2003 to 2006, 2,123 military personnel were treated for 'mental health conditions'. Of these, only 328 received diagnoses of PTSD.

Some facts and figures

It has been estimated that between 7 and 10% of the population in the UK suffers at one time or another from PTSD. These figures go up significantly in relation to the severity of the trauma suffered – according to some studies, among the highest trauma category (military personnel and rape victims) as many as 30% may experience PTSD. Some estimates suggest that as many as one quarter of the British armed forces personnel returning from Afghanistan and Iraq may experience some form of PTSD.

And, of course, the prevalence of PTSD isn't confined to the UK. In Canada, it is estimated that about one in eleven people will experience PTSD. Statistics Canada, the census and data collection agency in that country, suggests that about 7% of soldiers who deploy will develop PTSD. Another 4.5% will develop anxiety-related conditions, and another 13% will suffer from depression. The survey suggests figures of 2.8% of the general population and 7.2% for members of the armed forces.

In the US, approximately 7.7 million American adults, or about 3.5% of the population aged 18 and over, are experiencing PTSD at any given time. These include people who have experienced traumas such as rape, mugging, domestic assault, terrorism, accidents, natural disasters, and war. Reports claim that 19% of veterans from the Vietnam conflict experienced PTSD after returning from the war.

However, figures like these don't mean much to someone caught in the blitz of symptoms that make up PTSD. It might help to know that some very prestigious people have experienced what you're going through.

You're not alone

PTSD symptoms can vary from person to person, so if you compare symptoms you could feel alone. But you're not. Some famous and much admired warriors in history are alleged to have suffered from PTSD following their experiences in battle.

Winston Churchill, Britain's revered wartime leader, was known to suffer from intense depression, which he called his 'black dog'. But the prime minister also displayed symptoms of PTSD following a car accident in the United States.

Many historians believe that Alexander the Great was struggling with the symptoms of PTSD when he finally gave up his bid to extend his empire. Another warrior-leader, Indian emperor Ashoka (304 BC-232 BC) is said to have become so depressed after years of warfare, that he gave up military action and became a follower of Buddha.

Napoleon Bonaparte, the French emperor, committed suicide in 1821 after being banished to the Isle of St. Helena. It's believed that PTSD symptoms caused his depression.

American Nobel Laureate Ernest Hemingway, who joined the volunteers who fought in the Spanish Civil War in 1936, wrote one of his most famous books, 'Farewell to Arms', about his experiences. He suffered from acute depression later in life and committed suicide.

In more recent times, a Military Times photographer in Iraq photographed a young American soldier's rescue of a small Iraqi boy. The soldier was identified as Army Specialist Joseph Patrick Dwyer, and the photographs touched the hearts of many people around the world. Dwyer was a medic who heroically cared for the wounded on the battlefields of Iraq – but he could not heal his own wounds. Suffering from 'combat stress', the young man saw his marriage fall apart and found himself in conflict with the authorities as he turned to drugs for help in easing his symptoms. He died of an accidental drug overdose.

Summing Up

The long-term effects of a terrifying experience have been recognised for many years but it's only recently that the group of symptoms we now call post-traumatic stress disorder have been accepted as a diagnosis in the DSM-1V, the psychological diagnostic manual.

Unlike many other mental health problems, PTSD is triggered entirely by an external event. Just about anyone is vulnerable to PTSD if they experience a traumatic event stressful enough to be, or appear to be, life-threatening.

The symptoms usually appear shortly after the event, but in some cases only show up six months, or even several years, later. There is also complex PTSD which is the result of ongoing abuse or repeated trauma over a long period of time. This is often the diagnosis of adult victims of child abuse.

It is important to remember the definition of PTSD: The normal response of a normal human being to an abnormal event. It can happen to anyone – but the good news is that, due to ongoing study and research, PTSD symptoms can be alleviated and with time, cured.

Chapter Two

Developing Post-Traumatic Stress Disorder

One thing PTSD is not, is a sign of cowardice or weakness. People from all walks of life and cultures who have experienced a life-threatening or severely traumatic event have suffered from this disorder. There's no evidence that someone has to have a pre-existing vulnerability to mental illness, or have a weak personality, to develop PTSD.

In fact, all the evidence suggests that, unlike depression, obsessive-compulsive disorder (OCD), anxiety, or many other mental health problems which may be affected by your state of mind, the onset of PTSD is entirely based on stressful outside events. These may also be part of your PTSD symptoms, but in this case, they are a result of the external stress effect on you.

What do we mean by traumatic stress event? We don't mean not getting a promotion at work or being dumped by a lover. Sure, these are hurtful experiences and may result in depression, but they don't leave you afraid for your life or the lives of others. They don't have you fearing that you will undergo pain, disfigurement or torture, or that those you know and care about may be threatened. Unlike a PTSD trigger, these happenings are not so horrific you can't get them out of your mind and they do not imbue all your waking moments with fear and anger, while infesting your sleep with nightmares. They do not rob you of your long-term sense of safety, wellbeing, and of a future.

PTSD facts:

- Millions of people worldwide suffer from the condition.

- Women are more vulnerable to PTSD than men.

- It can strike at any age – even children.

- It usually follows a stressful, traumatic event.

- PTSD is not limited to military personnel who've been in battle – anyone experiencing a major trauma can develop the illness.

- With the help of a medical or mental health professional, PTSD can be cured.

The traumatic events which trigger PTSD are terrifying and shocking; they may range from a serious traffic accident to a violent mugging; from an earthquake to a battlefield: what they have in common is that they shake your sense of safety and security, and your trust in yourself and your society to keep you safe.

The condition's name comes from the science of pathology, where the word 'trauma' is used to indicate a wound or physical injury, and was adopted in psychiatry and psychology to mean a psychic injury which results in behavioural changes following a frightening event, or in some instances, an injury to the brain.

So – to use a widely accepted definition – 'PTSD is a normal reaction of a normal person to abnormal trauma or stress'. The human mind reacts to stress with a range of automatic or learned responses in an attempt to understand and cope.

In very severe stress or trauma, these coping mechanisms may be overwhelmed and unable to cope or come to terms with what the person has experienced. The natural self-preservation reactions don't switch off once the initial danger is past; the feelings engendered by the event, of terror, threat, danger and the need to escape, remain active in your brain and you're left in a constant state of high arousal, on guard, watchful and anxious.

Case study

'Anwar' had worked as a member of a fire-fighting crew for several years when he entered a burning building and saw a colleague hit by a falling beam. A short time later, he began to have nightmares in which he stood, frozen, watching his colleague plunge to his death, over and over again. Ironically, in reality the colleague survived the incident, although he was injured. But Anwar had been sure at the time the event occurred that his friend had had been killed, and this is how his mind repeatedly played out the event in his dreams.

PTSD is the mind's response to a wound – a non-physical wound, although the person may well have also suffered physical injury in the event – and is often referred to as 'an invisible wound'. It's fair to say that a person suffering from PTSD has been wounded by a terrible experience. However, they lack the physical scars and bandages that may help others understand that they are in pain. In this, PTSD resembles depression and similar mental health problems, because it's hard for someone to believe a person is in pain when they see no physical manifestations of it. As one woman, the victim of a mugging, said: 'The bruises from being knocked to the ground soon vanished, but the terror I felt just went on and on. I wasn't able to function, but everyone expected me to get back to my normal self, because they couldn't see anything physically wrong with me, like a broken leg or stitches. But I was hurting inside, all the time, afraid all the time, and couldn't make anyone understand.'

Who is at risk of developing PTSD?

To put it simply: we all are. Our day-to-day activities involve driving in traffic or crossing busy streets where life-threatening accidents can happen. We may be unfortunate enough to be the victim of a crime, or caught up in a natural disaster, such as seeing our homes or neighbourhoods destroyed by fire or flood, storm or earthquake. In other words, anyone can develop PTSD if the circumstances are right, i.e. experiencing a trauma that we identify as life-threatening. In some instances, witnessing a terrifying event can be enough to trigger the illness, even if you, yourself, were not actually physically injured or in danger.

Some common trigger events for PTSD:

- Witnessing or being a victim of violence.

- Being assaulted or mugged, especially a sexual assault.

- Being caught up in war, as a soldier, civilian or prisoner of war.

- Serious car, train, bus or plane crashes.

- Natural or man-made disasters, such as severe storms causing damage, hurricanes, floods, or fire.

- The sudden death of someone you love.

- A diagnosis of serious or terminal illness.

- Brain injury.

Sometimes, witnessing a traumatic event can trigger symptoms of PTSD – particularly if you are in a profession such as fireman, doctor, emergency room staff, police officer or other job where you may witness the results of a serious accident, violent crime, or war. For police officers and firemen, this risk may be intensified as their work may also put them in serious danger.

Does age affect the likelihood of developing PTSD?

Yes and no.

According to studies, there is no comprehensive and reliable evidence that a person's age has any direct impact on whether they will develop PTSD or not. That said, your age when you experienced a triggering trauma, combined with cultural, economic, social and historical factors in your background, may affect the way you react to trauma. Researchers found that people of different ages in different countries reacted differently; in some cultures older people were more likely to develop PTSD than younger people; in other countries this was reversed. The difference was possibly more due to their cultural backgrounds and social attitudes to age, rather than the age they were at when experiencing the trigger event. Put simply, the age you are when you experience the trauma affects the way you react consistent only with the culture you were born into.

Some people are more vulnerable than others

Some people can become more vulnerable to developing symptoms of PTSD if they have experienced previous severe trauma. Research also suggests that women are more vulnerable to developing PTSD than men – but also that they recover more quickly. This may be similar to the fact that women are more likely to seek their doctor's help in coping with other illnesses such as depression, while men try to 'tough it out' and are more reluctant to seek help.

It is also believed that some people have 'overreactive' nervous systems, because previous long-term stressful experiences have lowered their tolerance. This is the case with people who experienced physical and particularly sexual abuse as children – they may bury the pain and terror they have felt for years, and then a relatively minor incident may trigger PTSD because their stress levels were already elevated and so their tolerance or coping abilities were at a lowered level.

It is interesting that, just as everyone is an individual, so responses to traumatic events are individual. Some people who experience a terrible event develop PTSD while others do not. There are a number of studies underway by researchers who are trying to determine the reasons as to why some of us are more vulnerable than others to experiencing PTSD.

PTSD can occur weeks, months, even years after the event

Sometimes, the relief of having survived can carry us through the trauma of an incredibly frightening event. For example, people holidaying in Haiti during the earthquake of 2010 arrived back in their home countries filled with relief and happy to be back home and safe.

But psychologists warned that these people could well suffer from delayed PTSD once the euphoria of being alive and safe wore off and their minds were filled with the horrors they had seen – the bodies of the dead, the ruined buildings, the lost or injured friends, the sheer enormity of the tragedy they had left behind.

People in such situations may also suffer from 'survivor guilt', knowing that by some fluke they had escaped a terrible fate while others perished. They may agonise about why they survived and others didn't; sometimes they begin to believe superstitiously that somehow 'Fate' will pay them back for their good fortune and they develop extreme anxiety and watchfulness. For witnesses of vast tragedies, this is particularly so, as our television screens are filled with images, month after month, of the suffering of the people left behind as they struggle to get back to normal in a totally abnormal situation.

The Haitian earthquake or the 2000 tsunami were huge, almost cataclysmic events. But the same mechanisms hold true for smaller happenings: being a survivor of a motor vehicle accident in which others died; escaping the worst of a flood when your neighbours' homes were devastated; being held hostage and then released while others still remained in danger; even down to keeping your job when many of your colleagues were made redundant.

All these and similar situations can raise our sense of guilt at surviving and in turn cause the trauma we experienced to be repeated over and over in our minds, triggering PTSD once the event itself is over and we are safe again. And, being human, we tend to examine the 'might have beens': 'I might have been killed!' 'My child could have been kidnapped!' 'If my wife had been in the car, she'd be dead!' 'If I lost my job, we'd lose everything!' These thoughts trigger a sense of being unsafe, which is common amongst people recovering from traumatic stresses.

Summing Up

'PTSD is a normal reaction of a normal person to abnormal trauma or stress'. The human mind reacts to stress with a range of automatic or learned responses in an attempt to understand and cope. Your chances of developing PTSD are not affected by your age, your culture, or your state of mind at the time the event occurs – and PTSD can appear weeks, months or even years after the triggering event.

A triggering event is a very serious occurrence, usually with life-threatening implications, and being witness to such an event, especially if the lives of your loved ones are threatened, can be enough to trigger PTSD.

And it's not a question of being physically or mentally vulnerable – some of the heroes of our society – military, police, firefighters, disaster workers and medical personnel – are at high risk of developing post-traumatic stress disorder because of their work.

PTSD symptoms usually appear when the event is over, at a time when we might think the danger is past. In fact, not feeling safe again is one of the indicators of PTSD. For some people, it's compounded by 'survivor guilt' when they have seen others injured or killed and they have come through unscathed, leaving them to wonder why they survived when others didn't. There is also a sense that the threat is still there, waiting just around the corner to pounce again because, somehow, it missed you the first time around.

Because we're all individuals, our response to trauma is also individual and some people don't develop PTSD, even though others who have experienced the same trauma do. It's not a sign of weakness. PTSD is the result of a severe trauma which triggers the symptoms, and anyone of any age, race, or culture is vulnerable.

The point to bear in mind is that, with patience and proper professional help, PTSD can be cured.

Chapter Three

What Causes PTSD?

In PTSD, the symptoms are severe, wide-ranging, and involve a great deal of mental and emotional anguish which can translate into physical pain and ill health. With PTSD, the relief of feeling that 'it's over and I'm safe now' doesn't arrive. A PTSD sufferer experiences an ongoing feeling of threat, insecurity, fear, and physical reactions, almost as if the event had never ended – or could happen again at any moment. With PTSD, you do not feel safe again.

The more serious the event, and the longer its duration, the more likely those involved or witnessing it are to develop problems. The likelihood of PTSD increases when the traumatic event includes one or more of the following:

- It occurs without warning.

- It lasts a long time.

- It involves sexual assault or a physical injury, or a combination of both.

- The event happens again within a short time, or the person involved believes it's likely to happen again.

- Several traumatic events happen within a short time of one another and there's no time to recover from one before the next one arrives. An example would be an earthquake which causes buildings to collapse followed by aftershocks which cause further collapse. A similar effect would be a traffic collision where other vehicles plough into the first collision, or into rescue vehicles.

- Events which occur in childhood before a person's personality and coping abilities are developed can be particularly frightening.

For most people, the extremely stressful event, or triggering event, that results in PTSD comes in the form of one sudden, frightening occurrence in which they fear for their own lives or the lives of other people. PTSD is a reaction to that event – usually occurring once the event is over. As we said earlier, a 'normal reaction of a normal person to an abnormal event'.

PTSD can affect many people, including those we associate with heroism, such as firefighters, rescue workers, military and emergency medical personnel. PTSD isn't affected by your state of mind when the trauma happens; it is an illness caused entirely by external events which terrorise and traumatise you, and over which you have no control.

We're not talking here about the bout of 'the shakes' or nausea you might experience after a minor car accident or a nasty fall or similar scary happening. These are physical reactions that usually pass quite quickly once you feel safe again.

For someone suffering from PTSD, that feeling of being 'safe again' doesn't happen and they are left feeling isolated, angry, afraid and unable to move on with their lives.

Recognising the symptoms of post-traumatic stress disorder

We're all individuals with different thoughts, feelings and responses, so it's fair to say that not everyone reacts to trauma in the same way. However, there are a number of symptoms which do occur in PTSD and a diagnosis of the disorder, and the severity that you are experiencing, will come from the number and level of these symptoms you are experiencing.

First and foremost, though, to suffer from PTSD you must have been involved in a traumatic event. This is an event which, when it occurred, had you terrified, fearing for your life or the lives of other people. It can be anything from a serious traffic accident to a natural disaster, such as a hurricane or flooding; or you may have been the victim of a crime or caught up in a war zone under fire. While these sorts of disasters usually involve injury of some sort, you don't necessarily have to be physically wounded to develop PTSD.

Bearing in mind the definition of PTSD as 'the normal reaction of a normal person to an abnormal event', can you identify an occurrence that would have been serious enough to trigger your symptoms?

Here are some of the more readily identifiable traumas:

- A car accident involving serious injury or death, or where you thought at the time that these were unavoidable.

- A violent crime such as a mugging, assault, robbery with violence, home invasion, hostage taking, etc.

- Rape or sexual assault.

- Natural disasters, such as flooding, earthquake, tsunami, hurricane, tornado.

- Acts of terrorism such as occurred in the London Underground a few years ago, the bombings related to the Northern Ireland situation, or the bloody attack on the hotel in Mumbai.

- Man-made situations such as acts of war, whether actual battles or under sniper fire, etc., whether as a member of the military or a civilian.

- Ongoing severe bullying at work or at school

- Child abuse or domestic violence

Even witnessing one of these events can be enough of a trauma to trigger PTSD.

PTSD can occur some time after the triggering event

As we've said, there can be a delay in the onset of PTSD symptoms. In fact, there's a recognised type of PTSD that results from childhood abuse which is repressed and doesn't manifest until later in life. PTSD usually manifests itself within six months, but this varies from person to person. Certain forms of long-term stress, such as being involved in an abusive relationship or the victim of bullying at school or at work, can also act as a trigger for PTSD. We'll talk about these later in the book.

Symptoms of PTSD

You may be experiencing PTSD if you are having one or more of the following:

- Flashbacks, where you feel the traumatic event is happening all over again. You may even experience sights, smells and sounds that occurred during the event.

- Anxious or fearful thoughts or memories of the event, that intrude into your everyday activities.

- Frightening dreams, often replaying the event, sometimes with different sequences and endings.

- Distress, both psychological and physiological, on being exposed to situations that remind you of the trauma. This may be an unconscious memory.

- You feel emotionally numb, as though you are no longer connected even to those you care about, and you are perhaps unable to feel emotions such as joy or grief.

- You avoid as much as possible thinking or talking about the event or anything that might bring about a memory of the event.

- You find yourself unable to recall parts of the event that you think are important.

- You lose interest in doing things that you once enjoyed, including intimacy with your partner.

NB: This list is intended for guidance only. If you believe you may be suffering from PTSD, or if you have one or more of these symptoms, then you should consult your doctor or mental health professional. Doctors or mental health professionals are the only people qualified to make a diagnosis.

Types of PTSD

The first criteria for a diagnosis of PTSD is that you – the survivor, we'll call you – have had a traumatic experience, usually one severe enough that you believe your life was threatened, or that you were at risk of serious injury. This also includes a threat to someone else, particularly if that someone is one you care a lot about.

The second criteria is that the event caused you extreme fear, so much so that you probably still feel it when you think about what happened, along with an ongoing feeling of your own helplessness or powerlessness.

You may still be experiencing PTSD even if it's been some time since the event occurred. You might feel you've recovered and then, seemingly out of a clear blue sky, you get all these feelings of anger, powerlessness, fear, depression, apprehension, shame, guilt – feelings that other people who have not had the same experience may find difficult to understand.

Case study

Jack thought he had left the events of his tours of duty in Iraq behind. One day, in a shopping mall with his wife and young son, he was startled by a loud buzzing alarm. Jack threw himself to the floor and covered his head, imagining himself back on the streets of Baghdad under sniper attack. The embarrassing and distressing event prompted him to finally admit the frightening symptoms he was experiencing and to seek help.

PTSD without an obvious trigger

What if you're sure you have all the reactions of a survivor experiencing PTSD, but you can't remember a traumatic event that would have knocked you for six like that? You may still have the disorder – there are occurrences where PTSD can occur without a sudden event. One is called complex PTSD, in which the stress continues for a long period of time – victims of prolonged sexual abuse in childhood may develop this type of PTSD in adulthood.

Another, where PSTD develops as a result of a traumatic brain injury, is still being studied and the conclusions reached by researchers are inconclusive, although generally the findings do indicate the onset of PTSD following brain injury.

In addition, people who experience long-term bullying and humiliation at work, school, or in their personal lives – such as domestic abuse with or without actual physical violence – may develop PTSD without having one specific incident as trigger.

So, we know that PTSD is a normal reaction of a normal person to an abnormal stress, but you're probably asking 'Why does it happen?' Here are some of the explanations:

Why we get PTSD

You may hear the term 'hyper arousal' used in relation to PTSD. Someone with hyper arousal is unable to relax and feels the need to be constantly watchful and on guard, as if needing to defend him or herself from some form of attack or ambush.

Case study

Mark experienced PTSD after he suffered a violent home invasion which left him unable to relax or feel safe in a home he'd once loved. He had a security system with cameras fitted and monitored every activity around his home. Arriving home from work, he would go around the house carrying a cricket bat, checking each room for intruders. At night, after making several rounds of the house to check the locks on doors and windows, he would go to bed with the bat and his mobile phone on the pillow beside him. He stopped inviting people around to socialise, and stopped going out in the evenings as he was afraid to arrive home after dark. He eventually became afraid to leave the house for any period of time, and it was only after visiting his GP for various unexplained illnesses and anxiety attacks that he discovered there was a good explanation for his enhanced fears – he was experiencing PTSD.

Nature gave us – and most living creatures – a shot at survival by being able to choose to either run away or stand and fight when threatened. The choice depends on a quick, instinctive assessment of the circumstances, and is called the 'fight or flight' reaction.

Remember that although we've changed our lifestyles quite a bit since we lived in caves, there's a tiny bit of our brains which reverts straight back to those early days of evolution when we're threatened. Without getting too scientific, the adrenal gland starts to pump adrenalin or noradrenalin into your system, which makes you hyper aware (hyper in this instance means excessive). Your blood pressure, blood sugar and heart rate all rise, while your muscles tense in readiness. Your jaw tightens, ready to either scream or to keep you very quiet. If you're a man, your throat swells and the voice deepens to make you appear more aggressive and frightening to an opponent. If you're a woman, the effect is the opposite – your voice gets more high-pitched so that it's like a scream – which acts as an alarm signal to all the others in your tribe that you need help, pronto.

While all this is going on, your stomach is putting out acid to quickly digest its contents in case you need to run fast – which accounts for that nauseous feeling, or in more severe cases, stomach ulcers from prolonged stress. Even your eyes get in on the act – they narrow so that your peripheral vision improves to help you watch for attacks from the side or from behind you. Your shoulders tighten and draw up, making you look bigger and broader than you are.

So, when faced with danger, you're equipped to make a quick assessment and choose whether to fight or flee to save yourself. Of course, in evolution we have learned to suppress or moderate that reaction in line with what is expected of us in society.

When facing a threat of violence, we can size up our opponent and decide whether we have a good chance of fighting and beating him, or whether we should head for safety. In the dentist's chair, when our instincts may be saying 'Run!' as the drill approaches, our civilised selves accept that this is something good for us so we repress the fight or flight instinct in favour of a bright smile and healthy teeth.

We've learned how to negotiate our way out of trouble, or to suppress many of these instinctive feelings when faced with modern day dangers – for example, we don't run screaming from the office just because the boss is giving us a dressing down. Most people don't give in to the impulse to punch him, either!

But with the kind of event that causes PTSD, there usually isn't any action we could take to avoid the situation. We couldn't stop the earthquake that shattered our home, or predict that there was a car speeding towards us around the next bend with a drunk driver at the wheel. These are events that we are powerless to use our fight or flight reaction in.

The same applies to being caught up in war, whether as a member of the military or a civilian caught in the crossfire, we're stuck in the situation and whether we stand and fight or try to flee, there's a good chance that we'll be traumatised by the event. The trauma may be as great if we see other people shattered in a car wreck, or observe a fellow officer falling on the battlefield, as if it occurred to ourselves.

One of the more recently discovered facts about PTSD is that there is a difference in intensity of the trauma between events that we could call an 'act of God' such as a natural disaster, and those that are man-made, such as a criminal assault or war situation.

People may be more sanguine about 'acts of God' or nature, such as earthquakes, and recover more quickly because they still maintain their trust in other people and authority. But if the awful event is the result of a calculated action by someone else; such as a mugger, an enemy soldier or a drunk driver, or more broadly speaking, our government, there may be feelings of betrayal and of being unsafe which persist longer. This is because the person suffering PTSD feels betrayed by an apparent deliberate act by other human beings (or by society) with a resultant loss of faith in people, the authorities, and in society in general to keep them safe from harm. This distrust can become violent if other aspects of PTSD, such as flashbacks and anxiety, kick in at the same time a confrontation is taking place.

Again, the list opposite is not intended as a diagnostic tool, but if you – or the person you are concerned about – are experiencing any of these, visit a doctor and discuss your situation as soon as possible. Don't just wait for the symptom(s) to go away – they may, in fact, get worse.

Other symptoms of PTSD:

- Sleep difficulties.
- Irritability.
- Uncontrollable anger.
- Inability to concentrate.
- Constant watchfulness and overprotectiveness of yourself or your family and friends.
- Overreaction to sudden noises.
- Flashbacks.
- Anxiety attacks.
- Depression
- Nightmares or other sleep interruptions.
- 'Waking nightmares' when they feel they are revisiting the trauma even though, at another level, they know it is not happening in the present time.
- Feelings of being alienated from other people.
- Loss of interest in things that were once enjoyable.
- Sexual dysfunction.
- Inability to remember the events that took place in the triggering trauma, and this causes distress.
- Avoiding talking or thinking about the triggering event.
- Emotional 'numbness' or shutting down of feelings.
- Getting upset around anniversary dates connected with the traumatic event – people who were involved with the 9/11 bombings in Manhattan still find themselves upset and tearful or angry a decade later on that date.
- A sense of foreboding, or a fixed idea that something bad will happen to you soon and that you cannot avoid it.

Summing Up

The symptoms of PTSD are severe, wide-ranging, and involve a great deal of mental and emotional anguish which can translate into physical pain and ill health. With PTSD, the relief of feeling that 'it's over and I'm safe now' doesn't arrive. This is the key to many of the symptoms you may be experiencing.

People with PTSD often experience flashbacks or nightmares in which they relive the events, although sometimes they aren't 'seeing' what actually happened or the order in which events took place. This is one of the areas that counselling can help, by going over the triggering event and getting everything into proper order and perspective – like the fireman whose flashbacks always showed his friend dying in the fire, while counselling helped him to understand that his dreams were actually voicing his worst fears. His friend and fellow fire officer was actually injured but survived.

Symptoms include anger, constant watchfulness, anxiety and panic attacks, depression, sleeplessness (or sleeping too much). Avoiding intimacy, an inability to trust, a sense of emotional numbness (or rawness), a sense of alienation, inability to concentrate, reliving the event either through nightmares or through the possibly even more frightening flashbacks in which you can feel the emotions, sights, smells and sounds of the event as if it were actually occurring again.

These and other symptoms make PTSD a very frightening and serious disturbance which needs professional help to come to terms with. The help of family and friends is important too, and many PTSD survivors find great help and comfort in therapy groups with others who have similar experiences.

Chapter Four

How PTSD is Diagnosed

Many mental health problems, such as depression or anxiety, may be affected by a person's existing state of mind as well as outside events. However, the studies show that a person's state of mind when a traumatic event occurs, doesn't affect the likelihood of experiencing PTSD. This is highlighted in a study of WW2 soldiers, where soldiers with stable family, social and mental health backgrounds were compared to soldiers with pre-existing indicators of mental health problems. In both groups, some men developed PTSD, others didn't. Later studies have looked at victims of crime and found that the severity of PTSD in victims came from the severity of the crime – someone coming home to find they'd been burgled and the burglar is gone would have a less severe attack of PTSD than someone who was robbed and beaten at gunpoint.

So the important factor in developing PTSD is the degree of *external* stress or trauma you experience, along with the duration of the event, not your *internal* existing state of mind. Developing PTSD doesn't depend on your age, race, gender, level of education or social background.

It can't be emphasised enough that PTSD is not an indicator that someone was mentally ill or weak before the event – it is the event itself that causes the illness. So, subjected to enough trauma and stress, anyone is vulnerable to developing the symptoms of PTSD.

People often ask how does it feel to have PTSD? They worry that because they feel a variety of symptoms, they won't be able to get a diagnosis. As a general rule, PTSD starts within six months of a severe stressor, although it can happen later. You feel anxious for no apparent reason, depressed, guilty and angry. You may feel sad and believe you are grieving, as traumatic PTSD-causing events often involve a loss of some kind. You probably have flashbacks or nightmares about the event, and reactions out of proportion to anything that reminds you of what happened.

According to the 'bible' of mental health diagnoses, the Diagnostic and Statistical Manual of Mental Disorders, or DSM 1V, for short, these are the criteria on which a diagnosis is based:

■ You have been exposed to an event which involved actual or threatened death or injury, causing you to respond with panic, fear and feelings of helplessness.

■ You keep re-experiencing the traumatic event through dreams, flashbacks, sudden intrusive memories, or unrest when in situations that remind you of the event.

■ You show evidence of 'avoidance behaviour' – that you are emotionally 'numb' and lose interest in other people and in the outside world. You may avoid talking about or thinking about the event.

■ You experience physiological 'hyper arousal' – physical symptoms of the 'fight or flight' impulse that we talked about earlier – with insomnia, agitation, irritability or outbursts of anger that you can't control.

■ You have experienced the above symptoms for at least a month.

■ The symptoms you are experiencing have had a significant impact on important areas of your life, such as your ability to interact with others, enjoy a social life, or function at work.

NB: This list is intended for guidance only. If you believe you may be suffering from PTSD, or if you have one or more of these symptoms, then you should consult your doctor or mental health professional. Doctors or mental health professionals are the only people qualified to make a diagnosis.

PTSD survivors have also reported experiencing distress, both psychological and physiological, on being exposed to situations that remind them of the trauma, and avoid as much as possible thinking or talking about the event or anything that might bring about memory of the event. You may find yourself becoming agitated if you are unable to recall parts of the event that you think are important, or the sequence in which the events happened.

Other feelings may include a sense of being emotionally dysfunctional, such as being unable, or even afraid, to show affection or enjoy intimacy. Equally frightening may be a sense of foreboding or irrelevance about the future, perhaps even thinking you're not destined to live long enough to be bothered making plans.

PTSD triggers may vary from person to person

There are a number of 'stressors' which can trigger PTSD, and again it's important to remember that individuals have individual responses to these events. Studies suggest that about 25% of people exposed to severely stressful events may develop PTSD-related symptoms.

Researchers Charles Figley and Bonnie Green, (1994) have estimated that up to 25% of people exposed to the following trauma may experience PTSD:

- 2% of those involved in serious accidents.

- 25-30% of people experiencing a community disaster.

- 25% of those who lose a loved one in traumatic circumstances.

- 30% of veterans.

- 65% of victims of non-sexual assault.

- 84% of battered women in shelters.

- 35-92% of rape victims.

PTSD is, like depression and some other mental health issues, an equal opportunity illness. Studies of large groups of participants have found that neither race, sex, educational or income levels made any difference in whether someone would develop PTSD or not.

Conditions related to PTSD:

- Depression.
- Disassociation .
- Anger.
- Panic attacks,.
- Phobias.
- Addictions, such as alcohol and drug abuse .
- Eating disorders.
- Compulsive behaviours.
- Gambling addiction.
- Agoraphobia.

If untreated, these conditions in PTSD may lead to:

- Illness.
- Social dysfunction.
- Family break-up.
- Domestic violence.
- Assaults or violent, aggressive behaviour.
- Distrust or disrespect for the law.
- Unemployment.
- Homelessness.
- Suicide.

Because PTSD involves your emotions and there is a close tie between emotions and physical reactions, you may experience all sorts of aches and pains: diarrhoea, headaches, sore muscles and joints, rapid heartbeat and/or feelings of panic or fear, often of an undefined threat.

Living in this state of constant high arousal and watchfulness can be exhausting mentally and physically. Many PTSD sufferers try to self-medicate with too much alcohol or drugs (both legal and illegal) leading to dysfunction in their social, family and working lives as well as more severe health problems. Sadly, a study of people with PTSD shows there appears to be a strong connection between suicide risk and having experienced a trauma.

Summing Up

The important factor in developing PTSD is the degree of *external* stress or trauma you experience, along with the duration of the event. It isn't affected by your *internal* existing state of mind, nor by your age, race, gender, level of education or social background.

It can't be emphasised enough that PTSD is not an indicator that someone was mentally ill or weak before the event – it is the event itself that causes the illness. So, subjected to enough trauma and stress, anyone is vulnerable to developing the symptoms of PTSD.

There is a rather wide-ranging set of parameters for diagnosing PTSD, as it does vary from individual to individual. However, roughly speaking, this is what the doctors look for when reaching a diagnosis: a traumatic triggering event; re-experiencing this event through nightmares or flashbacks; feelings of panic, anxiety, and helplessness; you try to avoid thinking or talking about the event, and become upset and restless when exposed to situations or events that remind you of what happened; you feel emotionally numb, avoiding intimacy; you lose interest in the things that you once enjoyed; you no longer feel safe and become hyper aroused and watchful; insomnia; uncontrolled anger, agitation; these symptoms have been continuing for at least a month and have had a negative impact on your life.

PTSD symptoms make it difficult to function normally at work, at home or socially and can have serious consequences including domestic violence, relationship break-ups, job loss and homelessness.

Chapter Five

Different Forms of PTSD

Acute PTSD

A person with acute PTSD experiences the symptoms usually within six months or so of the traumatic event. He or she can identify an event so traumatic that it triggered the symptoms they are experiencing, even though they originally may have thought they had recovered from the initial shock.

Delayed Onset PTSD

In this, the symptoms occur later than six months after the stressful event, and may even occur years later. For example, we now hear of adults in their fifties and sixties who were victims of sexual assault or abuse as children who are now displaying the symptoms of PTSD.

Complex PTSD

This is a form of PTSD which results from long-term or repeated exposure to frightening or stressful events. Many researchers think that events that involve a personal or social trauma, or involve powerlessness or loss of control, where the victim sees no way to escape, are the greatest factors in complex PTSD.

Sources of complex PTSD include:

- Repeated sexual abuse, particularly ongoing in childhood.
- Domestic violence.
- Torture.

- Physical abuse.
- Ongoing emotional abuse.
- Long-term bullying at work or at school.

Complex PTSD is best described as a disorder of extreme stress. You may have this if you have been exposed to long term stress. People caught up in natural disasters, such as massive earthquakes or a tsunami, or in man-made disasters, such as long-running wars, where the effects of the trauma go on for a long time or occur repeatedly, may also suffer from this complex form of the disorder.

But it is the long-term stress which occurs in childhood as the brain and personality are developing that make a person most vulnerable to complex PTSD. To further complicate the issue some of the triggering events that occurred early in life may well have been forgotten or repressed, but can be retrieved and worked through in counselling. Recent studies have shown that ongoing stressors in early life – childhood to early teens – may create changes to the brain and to the levels of hormone production. These changes have been linked to dysfunctions in memory, learning abilities and ability to regulate emotions and impulses.

If you are an adult experiencing complex PTSD, be prepared to be patient as treatment will take longer – after all, it took a long period of stress and trauma to develop the problem. Accept that you will probably progress at a slower rate, with occasional backsliding, but keep in mind that you will start to feel better and more in control of your feelings and behaviour. It's best if your treatment is carried out with a trained trauma specialist who will be sensitive to your special needs.

It is also becoming accepted that long-term social stressors, such as bullying at school and in the workplace, can also result in PTSD. Another possible source of complex PTSD under study, is emotional trauma caused by repeated 'intimate' betrayals, such as infidelity in relationships followed by promises of fidelity which are then broken in a repeating cycle.

Partial PTSD

If you feel you are experiencing some of the symptoms we've discussed that indicate a PTSD diagnosis, but you don't think you fit with all of them, then it is still possible you are suffering from the disorder. This is called partial PTSD and these are the usual criteria required for a diagnosis:

- You have experienced a severe trauma.

- You've found yourself repeatedly reliving or re-experiencing the event, avoiding thinking or talking about it entirely, or getting into a hyper arousal state when the subject is brought up.

- The symptoms you're experiencing are seriously affecting your relationships, your ability to work, or to function in your everyday life.

- These symptoms have been ongoing for four weeks or longer.

Brain injury and PTSD

It could seem obvious that someone who has suffered an accident severe enough to result in traumatic brain injury might also then experience symptoms of PTSD. But memory loss is common in brain injury. Is it possible to experience post-traumatic stress about an event you can't remember? Some experts have held that this is the case and that memory loss resulting from the brain injury prevents the onset of post-traumatic stress disorder because the patient doesn't actually recall the traumatic event.

However, studies show that 13% of the people who suffer mild traumatic brain injuries also experience acute stress disorders, and the majority of these patients receive a diagnosis of PTSD for symptoms reported several months after the initial trauma in which they sustained the brain injury. There have been exciting discoveries in recent years about the miracle of human memory, and it now seems possible that someone with a traumatic brain injury affecting their memories of the stressful event may actually experience continuing symptoms of PTSD because they can't come to terms with the trauma they experienced – a trauma they don't remember but still feel the effects of!

According to a study done at the University of Washington School of Medicine, patients with traumatic brain injury who also experienced PTSD took longer to recover and were more likely to have impaired cognitive abilities in areas such as reasoning and problem solving, memory, attention and concentration and thinking. The researchers said that, while their study didn't include factors such as the duration of coma or post-traumatic amnesia, their work did suggest the possibility that brain injury worsened the symptoms of PTSD.

Combat-related PTSD

We mentioned earlier that we're hearing a lot about PTSD nowadays because of the effects of combat trauma on members of the armed forces serving abroad. While each individual reaction to severe trauma may be different, victims of 'man-made' traumatic events – and war definitely falls into that category – are likely to suffer the most severe forms of the disorder.

So we'll take a look at combat-related PTSD by itself here. Battle situations certainly fit some of the most important criteria for a PTSD diagnosis – often repeated trauma as soldiers go from battle situation to battle situation, long-term stress over the period of one or more tours of duty; someone under fire could certainly believe that they or those close to them were under threat of death or injury; an intense range of feelings from fear to powerlessness, anger and horror.

War is not only a physical trauma but an intensely emotional and psychological one. Not only that, but battle conditions dictate a behaviour that goes against all that we are taught in ordinary society: soldiers are expected to kill or wound others, to cause destruction of property, to be an instrument of terror to others who may be innocent bystanders, to make snap judgements that may result in serious consequences to the lives of others – and all while under threat themselves.

No wonder returning soldiers may experience flashbacks, nightmares, a sense of powerlessness, disassociation, rage, shame, and inability to experience close relationships. The effect of man-made trauma is to cause its victims to be distrustful of authorities that may be perceived as having betrayed them by placing them in this dangerous situation; it can also cause a fear of intimacy that infects all relationships from those with friends and family, lovers or children.

About 90% of all people killed in wars are non-combatant civilian women and children. It's important to remember that civilians also experience the terrifying trauma of military action and will experience the same range of symptoms along with a more intense sense of powerlessness as they are truly victims of being 'in the wrong place at the wrong time'. Numbered among these are the elderly, women and children who may not have access to shelter or medical treatment. Victims of rape are rated along with military personnel as experiencing the most severe effects of PTSD, and in some war theatres, rape is a commonplace weapon of terror.

Need2Know

These are some of the stressors that are experienced by people who have gone through war situations:

- Environmental and cultural shock.

- Having to adjust to climate changes, such as extremes of heat in the desert

- The noise of bomb blasts, explosions, guns firing, shouting and other battlefield noises.

- Chemicals, poisons, radiation, bacteria – such as the components of 'dirty bombs'.

- Exposure to infectious diseases either from weapons or to illnesses not found in their home country.

- Skin irritations and infections, either from exposure to chemical weapons or from too much intense sunlight or freezing temperatures or other conditions they don't normally encounter.

- Physical wounds.

- Sleep deficit.

- Heavy work with little rest.

- Malnutrition and/or dehydration.

- Witnessing the wounding or deaths of friends, fellow officers or civilians caught up in the conflict.

- Fear that is ongoing.

- Rage and/or a sense of helplessness at the events in which they are involved.

- Shame or guilt at actions they may have committed as part of their duties, including causing death or injury to others.

- Homesickness.

- Loneliness.

- Boredom.

- Uncertainty about the immediate future.

- Amnesia brought about by combat shock.

One of the difficulties of combat-related PTSD is that many soldiers are reluctant to admit to their problems because they fear loss of promotion opportunities or being branded weak or cowardly. However, after reading this, if you are a member of the armed forces, we hope that you'll realise that PTSD is a perfectly reasonable reaction to your experiences in battle. There's nothing cowardly or weak about it – you're suffering invisible wounds, wounds which are treatable. With help you can find your way back to a happy and fulfilling life. You owe it to yourself and to your loved ones to get the help you need.

Because of what we now know about the devastating mental, emotional and physical effects of war, it's vital that our societies provide properly funded and compassionate care and treatment of all the wounded, including those carrying the invisible wounds of PTSD. It is also important that civilians caught up in war are aided to rebuild their homes and societies as well as offered treatment for PTSD and other emotional and mental effects to prevent a new cycle of violence.

Summing Up

PTSD can manifest itself in several different forms, depending on the person and how the trauma was experienced. This is one area where age does have an affect: if you've experienced an abusive childhood (whether physical or sexual abuse), or the abuse has been long-lasting, you may develop complex PTSD, which appears much later in life. Sometimes this can be hard to diagnose as there is no obvious recent triggering event; however, the person experiences PTSD symptoms including nightmares or flashbacks which may point the way to childhood events. In some cases, these memories may be hard to unearth as the person has blotted them out and does not remember at a conscious level. This is sometimes called 'repressed memory'.

Other long-term stressors which can lead to complex PTSD include bullying, either at work or at school, and domestic violence.

It's also possible to experience 'partial PTSD' where not all the symptoms occur but the impact on the person's life is still quite severe.

Combat-related PTSD is perhaps the best known manifestation, and affects both military personnel and civilians caught up in war situations. PTSD appears to be most severe for people whose triggering event is in combat or in sexual assault.

There is also PTSD caused by brain injury, which is undergoing a lot of study at the moment. It can be quite controversial as to whether these patients are suffering from an actual physical damage to the brain which causes their symptoms, or whether the PTSD sets in as a result of the event which caused the brain injury. The research is further muddied by contention about whether someone who doesn't remember the event which resulted in brain injury (memory loss is quite common) can actually develop PTSD, which has flashbacks and nightmares of a triggering event as part of its diagnosis.

Chapter Six

Treatments for PTSD

Counselling

There are several treatment methods that are used with PTSD sufferers, with counselling/psychotherapy among the most effective and widely used. Medication is usually used to calm symptoms so that you can concentrate on the therapy.

The usual counselling treatment is cognitive behavioural therapy, or CBT. CBT helps a patient to understand his behaviours and thoughts, and then to change them. This is where exposure therapy comes in – by re-experiencing the event by talking or in pictures or on video while knowing you are in a safe place, you are free to express your fears, to face them and to control them. Once you are in control and understand that the event is past and you are no longer in danger, then you won't feel so overwhelmed and distressed or numbed.

Sometimes this is done by a technique called 'flooding' in which the patient is plunged into memories of the traumatic event all at once. A more preferable route, depending on the person and on the trauma they've experienced, is to start with smaller stressful events – remember that PTSD makes a person more sensitive to the kind of everyday stress that they'd generally brush off – and work up to confronting the major trauma. The latter technique is called 'desensitisation'.

During CBT therapy you will also learn:

- Breathing retraining or biofeedback skills to help you cope with anxiety and panic attacks.

- Methods for controlling anger.

- How to overlay negative thoughts with positive ones, and so change the way you think.

- How to prevent relapses into self-medication with drugs and/or alcohol.

- Communication skills to help you relate more effectively to the people around you, including family and co-workers. You may also undergo marriage or relationship counselling and/or counselling for addictions.

- Stress inoculation – a way of preparing for events that cause you stress so that you can cope with them.

Your counsellor will help you to recognise the signals that you are building up to a sudden attack of rage, or that your thoughts are heading towards suicide. She may also be able to help you using neuro-linguistic programming – a method of devising a 'signal' that a person can use to return to a calmer frame of mind.

Drug therapy or pharmacotherapy

Drug therapy, or pharmacotherapy as it is also called, involves using medication to help with depression, anxiety, insomnia and panic attacks that you may experience. For some people, the therapist may prescribe drugs that can help alleviate the emotional distress or numbness that goes with PTSD. Bear in mind that in most jurisdictions only a qualified medical doctor or psychiatrist can prescribe medication. Other therapists or counsellors may refer you back to your doctor with a request for prescription if needed.

While some antidepressants have been found to be effective for people suffering from PTSD in clinical trials, at the time of writing there is no definitive drug treatment for PTSD. The most likely use of drugs in your treatment will be to alleviate the effects of the symptoms you are experiencing so that psychotherapy or counselling are more effective.

These are some of the commonly prescribed drugs for PTSD symptoms. They should be prescribed by a doctor or psychiatrist as part of a treatment programme, and it should be remembered that many of these and similar drugs carry a risk of addiction.

Anti-anxiety drugs

Benzodiazepines such as Xanax (alprazolam), Librium (chlordiazepoxide), and Valium (diazepam) are prescribed to help reduce anxiety. Because they can be addictive they should only be used for short periods of time – less than two weeks.

Antidepressant drugs

Like Prozac (fluoxetine), Paxil (paroxetine) or Tofranil (imipramine) are prescribed for depression and anxiety and they help rebalance brain chemicals. They should only be taken under professional supervision.

Adrenergic agents

If you are experiencing hyper arousal, delusions, nightmares and flashbacks, your doctor may prescribe an adrenergic agent such as Catapres (clonidine), Inderal (propanalol) or Tenex (guanfacine).

Drug therapy should be used with care, as some do have side effects including drowsiness or addiction. Some antidepressants which can help reduce the intensity of PTSD symptoms and ease depression, have also been linked to feelings of restlessness or even suicidal thoughts in some users. If you are taking any of these drugs and feel you are having side effects, contact your doctor immediately.

These drugs may be listed under different proprietary names depending on the country you live in, but the chemical name will be the same. In some instances there may be generic drugs with the same composition that can be cheaper, so ask your doctor for recommendations.

Therapy groups

PTSD often leaves a person feeling totally alone and shut off from others because they feel that no one who hasn't been through their experiences can understand them. For this reason, therapy groups can be an excellent way for trauma survivors to talk freely about their feelings, fears and reactions to the trauma. It's easier to describe how you felt helpless and terrified for your life, or how you felt guilty as other people were injured or killed and you survived, when you know others in the room won't judge you because they, too, have been in your shoes.

The members of these therapy groups often form a cohesive and supportive network of people who can understand and empathise with and trust each other. In this environment, you can feel more confident in sharing your 'trauma narrative' and both be helped and help others in facing the grief, guilt and anxieties that may be dogging you. You are able to talk about these, and about the symptoms, nightmares, flashbacks, intrusive thoughts and memories, and feelings of panic that stem from your traumatic experience. This is a major step towards accepting what has happened and helping you to face and, eventually, overcome these symptoms.

In the military there are groups such as the Wounded Warrior groups in which soldiers who have shared similar traumatic events on the battlefield can understand, support and trust each other as they work their way through PTSD. If you have been in the military, you'll find the camaraderie of these groups comfortable as it is probably similar to your experience in your own battalion. The other participants in the group will have stories close to your own, and some may be on the road to recovery and able to share their experiences and advice.

When you listen to the stories other PTSD sufferers tell about their experiences and the aftermath, you will feel less alone and less ashamed because you can readily see that there is nothing abnormal or weak about your reaction.

Brief psychodynamic therapy

People suffering from PTSD often relive the traumatic experience over and over again, both in their intrusive wakening thoughts, in flashbacks and in nightmares. In these episodes, they experience the event as if it's happening all over again, feeling the fear and pain, hearing the sounds and the physiological sensations such as cold, sweating, shaking. Yet they find it hard to talk about to those closest to them for fear of being seen as cowardly, weak or mentally ill. In BPT you will be encouraged to tell your story and how it has affected you. Your therapist will be calm and non-judgemental, gently leading you to find better and more effective ways of thinking of the events. In this way you will build up your self-esteem and develop coping mechanisms and ways to deal with the intense feelings and emotions that resulted from the trauma. The therapist will also help you to identify and cope with situations in the present that trigger traumatic memories of the event and intensify your symptoms.

Eye movement desensitisation and reprocessing (EMDR)

This treatment is still under study at the time of writing, and may not be widely available. It's a promising treatment that uses exposure and cognitive behavioural techniques to redirect thoughts and attention. It also uses some elements of neuro-linguistic programming (NLP) in the form of eye movements, hand tapping, and various sounds. The idea is that you will watch the therapist's back-and-forth hand movement while focusing on images and feelings that are bothering you, or on negative thoughts. This is called attention redirection, and allows you to think about these things 'from a distance' while concentrating on something else. The issues that are worrying you become less threatening because of this 'distance' and so you are able to reach conclusions and solutions. Some therapists also use sounds or touch. However, as I said, this is still in its research stage, although it has been shown to reduce the symptoms of PTSD and is approved by the APA (American Psychiatric Association). You can find therapists who use EMDR through their international website (see help list at the back of the book).

Body-focused therapies

These therapies include physiotherapy and osteotherapy as well as massage, acupuncture and reflexology. They are aimed at easing the tension, anxiety, and hyper arousal – that feeling of always having to be on guard – that are so distressing in PTSD. Other body-focused therapies include meditation, yoga and tai chi exercises.

Hypnotherapy

Hypnosis can help you to relax, relieve stress and let go of harmful thoughts and feelings. In the hands of a skilled therapist, it can also help you to remember the events that caused you to be traumatised; you can perhaps recall the proper order of events and even things that you have forgotten that will help you make sense of what happened and to make peace with your feelings.

It's important to remember that, despite the vaudeville 'hypnosis' acts you may have seen on stage or television, you cannot be made to do anything under hypnosis that you would not willingly do, or that you are morally opposed to doing. So don't be afraid that the therapist will have you clucking like a chicken or dancing with a floor mop! Hypnotherapy can have a very relaxing and soothing effect which is beneficial to someone suffering from PTSD.

Herbal or 'natural' treatments

There are natural treatments that can help calm your nerves and soothe your anxieties, and these are being used effectively by some people with PTSD as an aid to relieving some of the PTSD symptoms. Do not, however, think that you can use these as an alternative to working with a counsellor, psychologist or psychiatrist as, while the herbal remedies may be soothing, they do not tackle the root causes of your problem.

Natural remedies include lemon balm and lavender, which help to soothe and calm the nerves. Some remedies, such as St. John's wort (also known as hypericum perforatum) have been shown to help lift depression and anxiety as they, like some of the pharmaceutical drugs mentioned earlier, help to balance the neurotransmitter chemicals in the brain. Generally, these remedies need to be taken over a period of time before they become effective. Check the dosages or get advice from a trustworthy herbalist – some brands do not contain high enough quantities of the herbal component to be effective.

Summing Up

While there are several treatment forms for PTSD, there is no quick-fix. Counselling and related therapies, such as hypnotherapy, neuro-linguistic programming, EMDR and body-focused therapies all require a lengthy period of treatment.

At the time of writing, there don't seem to be any drug therapies available for PTSD that achieve more than calming symptoms so that counselling treatments can be more affective. Drug treatments can help with symptoms such as panic attacks and depression, but it does seem that the best way to come through PTSD is to go over the events that caused it through counselling, developing a perspective and closure.

If you're experiencing PTSD you may feel very alone and isolated, as it is hard for someone who has not had your experience to relate to the feelings you're enduring. For this reason, group therapy can be very helpful. This is especially true for military personnel who are joining groups such as Wounded Warriors so that they can talk about their feelings with others who have been through similar traumatic events.

Chapter Seven

You Can Help
Yourself Get Well

If you think you are suffering from this disorder it's impossible to emphasise too greatly that you should make an appointment to see your medical practitioner immediately. The first step should probably be to get a full medical check-up to look for any underlying physical illness. This should be followed by a session with a mental health professional to determine a correct diagnosis and the degree of PTSD you are experiencing. From there you can work with your treatment team to decide on the treatment you need – this usually includes both drugs and counselling.

Don't try to 'tough it out' as, left untreated, the symptoms of PTSD can become increasingly severe and result in consequences that can cause you and your loved ones a lot of unhappiness. People with PTSD have found themselves alone as family ties break down, and unable to hold down a job or to function normally in society without professional help and support. The sense of betrayal may lead to trouble with the authorities.

All the indicators are that, without help, PTSD gets worse. Why put yourself through all that when there is help and a cure available? There should be no stigma involved, no reason to be ashamed of what you are experiencing because, as we said earlier, it is a 'normal reaction of a normal person to an abnormal stress'.

I cannot state strongly enough the advisability of getting professional help as soon as possible in order to return to a sense of wellbeing and self-worth. Help is out there, although in some areas it may be necessary to insist on being referred to a qualified psychologist, psychiatrist, or counsellor who can help you.

Taking that first step

Step one is to visit your medical doctor. Explain what has been happening to you and how you feel. Ask for a full physical check-up to make sure there's no underlying health problems. If there is, then follow through and get treatment. The healthier you are physically, the stronger you'll feel to deal with your PTSD!

With a diagnosis of PTSD, you should then get references to other professionals who will help, advise and guide you through the PTSD. Don't be afraid to seek a second opinion if you aren't satisfied with the diagnosis or treatment regimens offered by any of the professionals you will meet along your way to better health; taking control of your life and your PTSD is part of the healing process. Remember that each person is an individual and the symptoms, duration and treatment of PTSD vary from person to person with no one-size-fits-all diagnosis and remedy.

When you discuss your symptoms and experience with your doctor and other medical and mental health people you'll meet along the way, don't be afraid to list everything that you are experiencing. It may help to write things down before your visit – go so far as to print out a copy of your list and hand it over to the professional you are seeing. PTSD is an illness with many facets; there's no need to feel ashamed or a failure because of what is happening to you and, should any of the helpers you are referred to should make you feel that way, or make you feel like a malingerer, either complain to them or see your doctor for a referral to someone more competent.

You have been through a terrible experience, or series of terrible, frightening, stressful experiences and it's only natural to have difficulty coming to terms with your thoughts and feelings. Remember the definition of PTSD: 'A normal reaction of a normal person to abnormal stress'.

Things to tell your doctor:

- Describe the trauma you experienced.

- Tell him how you felt at the time, and the feelings and reactions that have followed.

- Explain how what is happening is affecting your life and your relationships.

- Don't be ashamed to mention feelings of fear, guilt, hopelessness, anger, or other emotions that may be swamping you.

- Do inform your doctor if you've experienced feelings of depression, uncontrollable anger or of the desire for suicide.

- If you are experiencing panic attacks, flashbacks, sleeplessness or bad dreams, tell your doctor this too.

- Request a reference to a mental health professional with experience in PTSD or similar conditions such as panic or anxiety disorders.

Step two: you've been diagnosed with PTSD – what now?

You've been diagnosed as suffering from PTSD. At least now you have a name for all these feelings, physical and mental pains, thoughts and reactions you've been having so much difficulty coping with. You may even feel a sense of relief that there really is something wrong and it's not all in your imagination. This is the time to consider your treatment options and to discuss all these with your doctor. Do your own research – there are lots of online sites and online support groups, and your local library probably has a drug encyclopaedia. Again, taking control of even this small part of your treatment will help empower you towards getting well.

Step three: coping with other people

You're still going to have to cope with people who will tell you to 'get over it' and get on with your life. Some people may try to stop you talking about your experience; others may seem pushy in asking questions when you don't want to talk. Others will try to avoid you – a weakness on their part because they can't cope with or understand your pain. People close to you may even be angry with you for 'not getting over it' and for the disruption your illness is causing in their own lives. A small number of those you know will suggest that you're weak, or even blame you for the situation you're in.

As we've mentioned earlier, because mental and emotional wounds don't show, some people find it hard to understand that they exist. Can you be patient and explain – possibly many times over – that this is a real illness and that you're trying your best to cope with it and recover? Otherwise you're going to have to try to either ignore thoughtless souls who think they're doing you a favour by trying to jolly you out of your 'funk', or else avoid these people as much as possible while you get on with your recovery programme.

Step four: the good news is that PTSD is curable.

The bad news is that it can take some time to get back to as close as your normal as possible. Take into account the reality that anyone who has experienced something as terrible as you have will be changed forever by the experience. But you can take the good from that change and let go of the bad. You will need to exercise patience with yourself as well as those around you, and that's not easy when you're probably feeling out of control of your own life. So the next step is to take some control back – learn as much as you can about PTSD. Reading this book is a good start, and there are other books and resources (some are listed at the end of this book). There is also a lot of information on the Internet, and we've included some of these links too. You'll also find online groups of people who are also trying to work their way through the painful and sometimes bewildering aftermath of trauma, and your doctor or counsellor may be able to help you find a group that you can join locally or you can join one online.

Step five: keep with the treatment

Whatever treatment path you choose, it's very important that you keep with it. Go to meetings, take the medication, be sure to turn up for counselling sessions or therapy group sessions, stay in touch with your professional helpers. And stay in touch with yourself, with your own feelings and what's happening inside your head. Learn to know when you're getting overwhelmed and to find some way to calm things down before the anger attack or panic attack hits you. Learn to recognise the danger signs, particularly if PTSD has had you flying into violent rages or considering suicide; knowing when these feelings are coming will help you to control them or seek help. These are the things that a counsellor can help you come to terms with.

You are a survivor, you've been through terrible things and survived; now is the time to gather your strength and work towards empowering yourself by taking an active part in your own treatment.

Step six: understanding yourself

This is another way counselling can help you. If you learn about yourself, who you are, you can begin to understand the ways in which PTSD has affected you. Take some time to study your feelings, understand your own needs and the things that help you feel better. Examine even your darkest thoughts and deeds, and your moods. What triggers them? What can you do to avoid or mitigate them? Discuss this with your counsellor.

Of course, any time you feel overwhelmed by these dark thoughts or moods, especially if you feel destructive or the need to hurt yourself, you should immediately call for help: your doctor, counsellor, hospital emergency service, or an emergency helpline (see the help list at the end of this book). Try to know ahead of time what you should do in this situation and keep a list of the relevant numbers where you can find it. Most of all, don't be ashamed to ask for help. You've survived a terrible experience. You have no need to prove your courage further.

Step seven: getting back into the world

This means making plans for your future, accepting the help and support of those who love you, whether family or friends. It means accepting yourself too, and believing that one day everything will come right again and you'll once more have that feeling of being safe and competent. Reach out to the people around you and try to understand that they may find your PTSD frightening or hard to understand. In helping them to understand what's happening with you, you'll probably find a greater understanding of yourself. The added support you'll receive from the people who are important to you – and to whom you are important – will help you recover.

Many people are finding that keeping a journal and writing down their thoughts and feelings helps them cope with PTSD, to see patterns in their reactions, and to find solutions. Additionally, writing things down gives you a good database for discussions with your counsellor.

Step eight: stop brooding and start doing

By this we don't mean get immersed in mindless, compulsive activity to avoid dealing with your problems. But when you are in the middle of mood swings, feelings of rage and despair, depression, anxiety and panic attacks, it can feel as though you are at the bottom of a deep, dark hole and, although you get occasional glimpses of the light above, escape seems impossible.

There are some ways to help yourself feel better. Exercise, with its release of endorphins (the feel-good hormones) will not only make you feel and look better, but will help to lift your mood and improve your physical health. Try jogging, walking, swimming – either alone, if you feel you can't trust your moods, or with friends or a group that gets together just for that activity.

PTSD can invoke feelings of uselessness and incompetence, of failure and a sense that there is no future for you. Consider activities that will lift you out of that feeling – perhaps planting a garden, helping with community projects such as building a kids' playground in your neighbourhood or helping an elderly or disabled neighbour. Volunteer at a local charity such as a soup kitchen – there's nothing like helping people in need to get a better perspective on your own situation. It also helps you to renew your sense of your own worth and competence – something that's important in recovering from PTSD.

Summing Up

If you think you are experiencing PTSD it is vital that you seek treatment. The first step for this is to see your doctor for a full check-up to make sure you're not suffering from any underlying physical illness that would contribute to your symptoms.

Your doctor should then refer you to a mental health professional for further consultation and diagnosis. You should discuss your treatment options and decide which is right for you. Although, whatever treatment you decide on needs to be given a reasonable trial, you should be prepared to try more than one option. This holds true with counselling, too: be prepared to ask a lot of questions and change counsellors until you find one who is a good fit for you. Do give each one a reasonable trial period, though – remember that you will probably have some resistance to baring your heart and soul in counselling and don't give in to the impulse to blame the counsellor and give up.

That said, you'll feel better participating in your own treatment, which involves everything from keeping appointments, getting regular exercise, eating a healthy diet, not abusing drugs or alcohol, and trying to get back into participating in your own community and family.

It's important to understand that all treatment methods require time and patience, but the result – a you free of the PTSD symptoms – will be well worth the effort.

Chapter Eight

Finding the Right Treatment

Keep in mind as we go through this chapter, that PTSD is a medically recognised anxiety disorder and it is a quite normal condition for any person who has undergone serious trauma and stress.

Because the experience of PTSD is very individual, it is important that any treatment course you take is tailored to your specific needs and symptoms. Because drug therapies appear to be less effective than counselling and psychotherapy, it's likely you will be referred to a counsellor or to a therapy group. However, the first thing that should happen when you are referred to a specialist is that he or she does a detailed evaluation. This will clarify the level and severity of your illness, and also your state of mind at the time.

If you are still in a traumatic situation – for example, you are homeless or still experiencing domestic abuse or bullying in some form, then it's important that steps are taken to remove you from that situation. Also, if you are using drugs and/or alcohol as a form of self-medication, your specialist will refer you for detoxification treatments.

It's not unusual for PTSD sufferers to be in a crisis condition when they are referred for treatment, which may involve serious depression or suicidal thoughts, or experiencing disorganised thinking or severe panic attacks. These issues must be stabilised or resolved before your treatment can begin effectively.

PTSD sufferers complain often of feeling powerless and also of feeling cut off from others. If you actively participate in your own treatment – starting with taking the first step of seeing your doctor – you'll begin to feel a little better. If you can also harness the support of your friends and family, and of others who were involved in the same traumatic event that was your trigger, then you will feel more in control and less alone.

During treatment, you'll probably be invited to bring your family members to a counselling session so that they can learn how PTSD happens, who gets it, how it affects you and those close to you, and other problems that are known to occur when someone experiences severe trauma. The understanding and support of people around you is a valuable component in helping you get through this, and they need to know that what you are experiencing is a normal reaction to a terrible trauma.

What to expect in treatment

The next part of the treatment will depend on the evaluation that your specialist has carried out, but may take the form of showing you pictures or video of events you experienced, or some that are similar. Don't panic at this idea – the point is that you can re-experience the event in a safe environment in a more detached manner because you are watching what happens while knowing that it is not actually going on now. This provides an opportunity for you to consider your own reactions and beliefs about what happened and your own role in it and discuss these with your therapist. Your therapist won't take you into this until she thinks you are ready.

Yes, you can get well

To begin to recover from PTSD you need to overcome the feelings of anger, shame, guilt and fear which thread through your experience. These are common feelings among survivors of terrible events.

Case study

I was part of an aid mission abroad, and we were caught in some severe flooding. A lot of the local people died or were left starving and homeless, but we were rescued. I remember a sense of euphoric relief – I was saved! Then the guilt set in: why was I saved, and so many of the people I was supposed to be helping died? I began to have nightmares about the bodies I'd seen in the water, and out of the blue, in the middle of my regular daytime activities, I'd flashback. Worst of all was a feeling that somehow I'd have to pay for my survival – that something bad was going to happen to me or my family to 'balance' the universe.

Tom, a volunteer aid worker.

Your therapist will help you to examine all these feelings and the memories you have of the event, your reactions and intrusive thoughts. Because you are doing this in a safe place with someone who understands what you are going through, you are less likely to become overwhelmed or experience the emotional numbness which may have dogged you when you were trying to cope alone. Your therapist will encourage you to trust him, and will guide you safely through times when your thoughts threaten to overwhelm you.

If, having read all the information so far, you think you may have PTSD, I can't emphasise enough the importance of getting a professional diagnosis and help.

Working with a counsellor

Counselling is usually the main form of treatment for PTSD – talking about your feelings, identifying the cause of your stress and learning coping skills are all vital to getting you back to health again. We'll use the term 'counsellor' here to denote the mental health professional you may be referred to or choose to work with, although this person may have any of a variety of qualifications including psychiatrist, psychologist, counsellor, or specialist in PTSD or similar disorders.

As with your visit to the doctor, it's best to be as open and honest as possible with this counsellor, to give her the broadest and most accurate picture of how PTSD is disrupting your life.

Some questions to ask when you have your first session with a counsellor:

- What is PTSD?

- How do you work with clients suffering from it?

- What experience do you have working with people going through what I'm experiencing?

- What treatments do you think are best for PTSD? Can you explain your methods, i.e. cognitive behavioural therapy.

- How long do you think I will need treatment?

- Do you recommend the use of drugs, and if so, what would you suggest?

- Are there any treatment methods that you think I should avoid?

Talk in depth about your feelings. Tell your counsellor what happened (the initial triggering trauma) and how you felt at the time. Do you feel more disturbed now than you did when the event first occurred? Are you experiencing flashbacks, bad dreams, sleep disorders? What effect is this having on your family life, or your close loved ones and friends? Have you become unable to function at work? Talk about your thoughts or fears about the future.

Tell her if you are experiencing sudden, uncontrollable rage, feelings of anger and/or violence, or thoughts of hopelessness and suicide. Your counsellor will be aware that all these things are common to people suffering PTSD, and is not going to judge you or think you weak or a coward. There is no need to 'tough this out' – remember, it can take a lot of courage to admit to needing help, too.

Choosing a counsellor

We should note at this point, that it is important that you find a counsellor with whom you are comfortable, someone you feel you can trust and speak freely with. As with people in other walks of life, you may not feel particularly at ease with one counsellor, and immediately comfortable with another. This is your life and it is important for you to find the best possible help for PTSD in order to get well as soon as you can; therefore it is important that you be happy with the professional who will accompany and aid you on this journey. Don't feel it will offend her if you ask for a referral somewhere else; a professional counsellor knows that it's better for both of you to 'have a good fit' if you are to work together and accomplish your goals.

Choosing the right counsellor for you. Don't be afraid to ask questions and take into account that:

- Some counsellors have very busy practices – will he be able to give you an early enough appointment or is there a waiting list? Will you be able to get appointments at a time that's convenient to you?

- Is the counsellor accredited in a way recognised by your medical insurance provider?

- How much does he charge – and is it affordable for your budget?

- If cost is a problem, does he have a sliding scale of fees geared to income?

- Don't be afraid to ask about credentials.

- Do you feel comfortable with this counsellor? Do you feel he lets you speak freely without interrupting you? Do you feel he 'reflects back' correctly what you are saying?

- What style of therapy does he practice? Can he explain his style and how he feels it is suited to your needs?

- Asking for references is problematic – counselling ethics stress confidentiality and so he can't give you the names of other clients to talk to.

It is important that you feel 'safe' with this person and that you are sure he will not betray any confidences. I always tell my clients that 'whatever is said in this room stays in this room. You can cry, laugh, get angry or say things that embarrass you or make you feel guilty and no one except the two of us will ever hear of it.' However, there may be some occasions you will want your counsellor to speak to your doctor or another health professional, and many counsellors will ask you to sign a waiver to allow that should the need arise.

What happens in counselling?

The counsellor will encourage you to discuss your feelings and experiences and use a technique called 'active listening' in which he will listen quietly and only speak to encourage you or to help you clarify a thought by reflecting back what you have said. He may sit quietly, without speaking, during your silences. Don't be alarmed at this – your counsellor is simply giving you time and space to consider and examine the issues you are talking about.

Many counsellors also teach relaxation techniques as well as working with you to improve communications, interpersonal relationships, anger management and addiction control, if needed. These are important coping mechanisms which will help you return to your everyday life without feeling isolated or 'different'.

It may be that, after several sessions with one counsellor, you feel that you have not built up the trust and rapport you need for counselling to be effective. Don't be afraid to discuss this with her; after all, you're there to talk about how you feel! If you do not think you can be comfortable talking to this mental health specialist, or if you feel you are being judged or hurried along, or any other issue that comes up, do either ask for a referral to see someone else, or visit your doctor and ask him to recommend another therapist. This is your treatment, a treatment aimed at empowering you – take control by making sure you are working with someone you feel comfortable with and can trust.

Eight things you can do to help yourself recover:

- Exercise.
- Get enough sleep.

- Eat a nutritious and well balanced diet.

- Drink water and stay hydrated.

- Learn relaxation techniques.

- Learn to communicate, especially with your partner, spouse, or nearest and dearest.

- Learn anger management techniques.

- Learn how to visualise yourself into a 'safe place' when symptoms strike.

Nine things to avoid:

- Cut down on anxiety-inducing caffeine and nicotine.

- Avoid alcohol and 'recreational' drugs.

- Don't try to repress or bottle up your symptoms and emotions.

- Avoid situations which make you tense or anxious whenever possible.

- If you've been prescribed medication, don't stop taking it without being advised by your doctor or mental health professional.

- Avoid extreme thinking.

- Avoid beating yourself up about things that aren't your fault or are outside your power to change.

- Don't shut yourself away from friends or family – social support is important.

- Don't miss appointments with your doctor, counsellor or psychiatric advisor.

What happens in hypnotherapy?

First and foremost, put out of your mind all those music hall comedy acts where someone is 'hypnotised' into doing odd or embarrassing things for the amusement of the audience. That's not what this is all about, and your therapist will probably explain that you cannot be hypnotised into doing anything that your conscious mind would consider wrong or immoral, anyway.

Hypnotism is just a deep state of relaxation – you may not feel as if you're asleep, but you'll probably find yourself feeling quite refreshed at the end of the session. You may not be consciously aware of everything that happens during your session, and some therapists record the events so that you can listen and discuss later.

Hypnotherapy has two objectives: 1 – it can be a way of revealing events or chronology that your conscious mind has forgotten or repressed and 2 – your therapist can make suggestions to your subconscious mind that will help you deal with problems and heal. Remember that you can't be hypnotised into doing anything you don't want to do!

Usually, the therapist will explain what is about to happen and get you sitting or lying, comfortably. She will answer any questions you have and then talk you through relaxation exercises. At some point she may suggest you close your eyes, or this may happen quite naturally. Once you reach quite a deep state of relaxation, the actual therapy will begin. This will usually take the form of asking you to describe in detail what happened, perhaps including things you have forgotten at a conscious level. The therapist may then make suggestions to you for calming anxiety or other symptoms. This may take the form of neuro-linguistic programming, where you will be asked to remember a happy, calm time. Then this happy, calm feeling will be tied to a gesture – perhaps touching a finger to your forehead, or tapping your knee. Then you will be told that when you feel an anxiety attack or other symptom that distresses you coming on, you touch your forehead or tap your knee to activate that calm, happy feeling again. Yes, this does work!

Summing Up

For many people, the processes of counselling and hypnotherapy are somewhat mysterious and can be a little frightening, which is why we've spent time in this chapter discussing what to expect.

It's important that, whichever practitioner you choose, you feel comfortable with him. Trust is a vital component of counselling – how can you bare your most raw feelings and fears to someone you don't trust? And that's what is needed in counselling. You have to be honest about what's going on with you so that your counsellor can help you not only work through the painful experience but also learn coping skills that will aid your recovery and help you in the future.

Hypnotherapy is used in counselling to help you free memories which may have become confused, hidden or repressed. The counsellor can then help you work through these and put everything into perspective. Some counsellors are also hypnotherapy practitioners and some aren't, so be prepared to be referred to another therapist if hypnosis seems right for you. Hypnosis itself is safe and can be a pleasant experience when carried out by a professional therapist – forget all those stage tricks where people are 'hypnotised' into doing embarrassing things! This is not what happens in hypnotherapy. Besides, you can't be hypnotised into doing anything that your conscious self would consider wrong or immoral.

Explore all the various treatment possibilities, don't be afraid to ask questions, and remember that taking part in your own treatment is a healing empowerment.

Chapter Nine

Explaining Some of the PTSD Terms

PTSD involves a wide range of behaviours, thoughts and feelings which you may find very distressing, and which may be distressing to those around you. Here, we are going to look at some of these:

Flashbacks

They come out of nowhere. You're busy getting on with your day, perhaps on the bus to work, relaxing with friends, doing the grocery shopping, and without warning your mind whisks you back to the scene of the triggering trauma and, for a few moments, you think you're actually going through it all again.

No, you're not going crazy. Flashbacks are your mind's way of telling you that you need to recognise and deal with what happened. Perhaps you've been suppressing the awful memories of the 'bad thing' that happened to you, walling them off from your present. Now they're back, in glorious Technicolor, transporting you, without warning, to the past events you've been trying to escape.

These are called 'disassociative flashbacks' because your mind is trying to dissociate, or separate, from the event that caused your PTSD. Flashbacks may be stronger if you have used 'recreational' drugs in the past, or are doing so presently. Sometimes they remain in the realm of a simple re-experiencing of the occurrence, but all too often they may elicit a violent response because they are so real – you react as you would if the event were happening all over again. That's why we sometimes hear stories of PTSD victims who, in the grip of a flashback, attack an innocent family member or bystander in the mistaken belief that they're defending themselves from a mugger or an enemy soldier. Sometimes there's a trigger – a car backfiring or a firework that sounds like gunfire, or sudden shouts or jostling that are a reminder of some other threatening event.

This can be embarrassing enough, but even more so as the person may not remember experiencing the flashback and so finds it hard to explain their behaviour. If you can trust the people around you enough to explain to them that you may have flashbacks to certain events, then they can offer you help and support.

Remember that flashbacks are your mind's way of bringing your attention to issues you need to deal with. Once you begin to work through the traumatic events and begin to accept what happened to you, your own actions and reactions, then the number and vivid nature of your flashbacks should lessen and eventually cease.

Anxiety attacks

PTSD is listed in the category of anxiety disorders because it has many similar symptoms to other anxiety-based disorders.

We talked in an earlier chapter about the 'fight or flight' arousal that is set in motion when we believe we are under a threat. Usually, when we are sure the threat has passed, our mind and body's reactions return to normal.

But the trigger mechanism for PTSD is so severe that our minds tell us: *It's not safe yet! Keep alert! Keep worrying!* We remain on full alert because we are still processing the fear-filled experience. This constant state of arousal affects the nervous system, leaving us sensitised to the point where even the slightest sign of alarm sends us into full fight or flight readiness.

It becomes a 'catch-22' situation, our bodies and brains never 'stand down' from the hyper arousal state, so we are always anxious and worried even though there is no threat to deal with. We tend to overreact to even trivial worries or problems, with the result that we're constantly frazzled. We suffer from the physical effects of this: fatigue, trembling, nausea, digestive upset, hyperventilation, rapid heartbeat, a sense of suffocation – and these lead to panic attacks.

These are just the physical aspects of anxiety. Emotionally, we're easily irritated, moody, constantly fearful and lacking in self-confidence. We feel confused, indecisive, and find it hard to concentrate. In-between the bouts of hyper arousal when we're panicking, we feel discouraged, depressed and hopeless.

The natural response is to avoid all the things, places, people and situations that seem to trigger our anxieties. For some people, this means never leaving home! But the way to cope with anxiety disorders is to face the fear. I know that's easier said than done, but you can slowly allow yourself to experience the stress and fear. Your mind and body will begin to accept that the fearful time is over and you can relax, winding down from the constant state of hyper arousal.

This is not something you should attempt alone. Talk to your counsellor or your therapy support group leader and get help to safely face and conquer your fearful feelings.

Numbing

We all have different ways of 'numbing' emotional or mental pain. For some, it's simple denial; for others it's alcohol or drugs. Some people bury themselves in work, others refuse to feel anything.

These are all, at best, temporary solutions; at worst, they make the situation worse and compromise your health, wellbeing and relationships. In the end, no matter how you deny your PTSD symptoms, someday all that bottled up fear, hurt and rage will emerge and demand that you deal with the issues behind them.

You should also consider the effects of your denials on those around you. Your family and marital relationships will flounder if you are unable to enjoy affection or intimacy; and for many people the misuse of drugs or alcohol can lead to break-ups in marriage or worse, domestic violence.

Drugs and alcohol will affect your health, your ability to maintain relationships, your ability to be part of your community, to hold down a job. You'll find it increasingly difficult to function in your social and work environments. Before you find yourself on that slippery slope to ill health, unemployment, poverty, homelessness and loneliness, get help from your doctor, counsellor or therapy group leader. Go to Alcoholics Anonymous or a drug rehabilitation group. They won't judge you – they've been where you are – but they will offer support, advice and help.

Another form of numbing is called 'alexithymia'. This is basically shutting down your feelings and emotions to avoid further hurt. By refusing to feel anything at all, you avoid feeling the pain of your triggering event. But the flip side is that you become robot-like. People with alexithymia refuse to admit they have a problem, but in refusing to feel the pain of their traumatic experience, they also shut down their ability to feel joy, love, pleasure, hope, empathy – or to experience affection and intimacy.

You can imagine what this does to a person's relationships. Unfortunately, people with alexithymia will deny that there is anything wrong, to the point of claiming that they were unaffected by the terrible events that caused their PTSD.

This makes it difficult for them to open up to a counsellor and it may take an intervention by a close friend or loved one to get them to seek the professional help they need in facing their residual pain and fear. However, this is the only way to 'open up' and unlock their feelings.

Hyper vigilance

This is sometimes called hyper arousal. This is a state of being on constant alert, of looking for and expecting something awful to happen at any moment. The result is often aggressive behaviour, of irritability with friends and loved ones, and a dysfunctional attitude towards the world which seems to have become an unsafe and frightening place, a place that cannot be trusted.

Case study

I insisted that the TV repairman show me his credentials before I'd let him in – even though I had called for service. I sat in my armchair, with a baseball bat leaning against the chair arm, and watched his every move, just waiting for signs that he was going to attack me like the two jerks in the bar had done. I wasn't going to fall for that nice guy act, oh no! Then I saw the way he was looking at me – he was afraid of me! At that point, I knew I was acting crazy and had to get help.

Mark.

Hyper vigilance, or excessive watchfulness, results from your mind's inability to close down the 'fight or flight' reactions and accept that you are now on safe ground. This can make you edgy, irritable and act in ways that may make others think you are downright odd or even paranoid. This puts a strain on every aspect of your life, and all the people in it. Talk to your counsellor – for many people, hypnotherapy can be a great help in relaxing the need to be hyper vigilant.

Anger management

The event that triggered your PTSD was very intense and frightening, so it's no small wonder that you feel a range of strong emotions which may result in erratic behaviour which can be very disturbing to those around you. Anger is one of these – you may, indeed, find your capacity to fly into sudden rages quite frightening – imagine how those around you feel! Your counsellor can help you to identify possible triggers and to learn techniques to control anger.

Identifying your emotional state

One of the ways you can help yourself is to know how you are feeling and to identify the 'triggers' which may send you running for cover, into a sudden rage, or into tears, a panic attack or flashback. Many people find it useful to write down the things, people, places and situations, and even food and drink that immediately precede a burst of intense emotion.

This can help you to avoid situations that will lead to problems, or to at least have some control by knowing ahead of time that you need to regulate your feelings. It also shows you in black and white whether you are overindulging or self-medicating with alcohol or drugs. If you need a few beers or pills immediately after (or before) a situation or event, then you know you have a problem.

Case study

I'd been involved in a train wreck in which I broke my leg, but some people died. We were trapped for several hours, so I thought I was doing well to be back at work and it didn't seem a big deal that I needed to pop a couple of tranquilisers before I got on the commuter train each morning. Then I needed to stop for a few beers before I got the train home, and even that didn't stop me having panic attacks. Even so, I thought I was coping. Then I needed more tranqs to get on the train, and the few beers on the way home became a few at lunchtime, too. Still I thought I was doing my best to cope – until my boss called me into his office and said if I didn't do something about my drinking, they'd have to let me go. Guess I wasn't coping at all – my therapist said I was self-medicating with the tranquilisers and booze .

Jim, 43

Keeping a record of your emotions and being aware of what's happening with you by pausing now and then and taking your emotional pulse, you can stop some problems before they start and identify problem areas which can produce fruitful discussions with your therapist.

Summing Up

It takes a very frightening and stressful incident to cause PTSD, so it's only to be expected that the emotions which follow can be very intense and often quite dark. It's not easy to cope with the artefacts left behind by the event: anger, fear, anxiety, panic attacks, nightmares, flashbacks, hyper arousal or hyper vigilance which leaves you constantly watchful and on guard.

Sometimes these emotions and fears can lead you into behaviours that people around you may find disturbing or frightening – bear this in mind when dealing with family members, especially children.

You can help yourself by identifying your emotions, and keeping a journal of events and feelings. This will help you to identify triggers – situations that may cause outbursts of rage, fear, panic attacks or flashbacks. It can also highlight situations that involve overindulging or self-medicating with alcohol or drugs (prescription or illegal). Take your journal to counselling sessions or to your group for discussion.

The pain and anxiety that feeling your emotions are out of control can create, is a major inducement to getting help. And help is available – your doctor, therapists and therapy group members can all offer help and support in getting your feelings back under control again. Don't be afraid to talk about what's going on with you and ask for help.

Chapter Ten

Post-Traumatic Stress Disorder in Children

It was once thought that children did not experience some of the mental health problems known to plague adults: these include depression, anxiety, and PTSD. The symptoms may present in slightly different ways in young children and teenagers.

Some symptoms to watch out for are:

- Repeated instances of re-enacting the event, through games, drawing, play acting or story telling.

- Bad dreams or night terrors.

- Being afraid of the dark.

- Problems falling asleep, sleeping too much, or waking up frequently during the night.

- Bed-wetting (in children who were previously toilet-trained).

- Sudden fears, such as of monsters under the bed, starting after the stressful event.

- Fear of being separated from a parent or close family member.

- Becoming irritable or unusually aggressive.

- Difficulty concentrating, remembering or focusing.

- Forgetting skills they have already learned.

- Becoming 'jumpy' or startling easily.

NB: This list is not meant as a diagnostic tool; only a doctor or mental health counsellor is qualified to diagnose.

Children often find it difficult to talk about their fears, and may insist that everything is all right when parents question them. Unlike adults, they are also unlikely to confide in their friends because they are afraid they'll be laughed at. Younger children may be unable to talk about the way they feel because they lack the necessary vocabulary. PTSD has been diagnosed in children as young as five years old.

Child psychologists are specially trained to help children express their feelings and fears. They use age-appropriate treatments which may include play therapy, drawing, using art equipment such as clay, or studying the way a child plays with various toys. These tactics can be used to get a child or young person to talk about their feelings and also to teach coping skills.

What causes PTSD in children?

The causes are more or less the same as those in adults, bearing in mind that a child cannot always interpret events in the same way as an adult with wider experience might. However, there is usually a triggering event which makes the child very afraid for herself or for someone close, such as a parent.

The major stressors for children often include bullying or physical or sexual abuse. In this case, often the adults involved are dysfunctional and so the child has the added burden of not having role models of healthy relationships. Children growing up in such circumstances often display a number of behavioural problems as well as the PTSD.

Behavioural problems in children and teenagers as a result of childhood abuse:

- Eating disorders.
- Alcohol abuse.
- Drug abuse.
- Aggression.
- Sexual maladjustment.
- Lack of impulse control.

82

- Self-destructive behaviour.

- Uncontrollable anger.

- Depression.

- Panic attacks.

- Amnesia.

- Difficulty thinking straight, scattered thoughts.

- Shutting themselves away from others, disassociation.

If these go untreated in a young person, he or she may be vulnerable to developing PTSD years later in adulthood following a relatively minor triggering event. Adults who have experienced childhood abuse and are diagnosed with complex PTSD usually have a range of problems from depression, personality disorders, anger and disassociation, as well as problems with close relationships.

As with adults, the risk of developing PTSD in children depends to a degree on how severe the trauma is – bearing in mind that the child may interpret something as being more serious that an adult might. Additionally, a child's likelihood of developing the disorder is affected by how his parents react – if they are obviously traumatised or very upset by the event, then the child will be more greatly affected. Children who have strong family support may cope better and have less severe PTSD symptoms.

Other components of PTSD in children that mirror those in adults:

- A child who witnesses 'man-made' traumatic events such as assault, drive-by shootings or rape, where one person is deliberately hurting another, is more likely to develop PTSD than if the event is a natural disaster – again, very similar to the experience of an adult.

- The more traumas a child experiences, or the longer the duration, the more likely the onset of PTSD.

- Girls are more vulnerable to developing PTSD than boys.

- The age a child is when they experience the trauma may not necessarily be a factor – research is ongoing – but the way they display the symptoms may vary according to their age.

Children of different ages show different symptoms

Children aged 5-12

Children in this younger age group don't seem to suffer from flashbacks, although they may well have nightmares. They are usually able to relate what happened, but often get the events or the chronology wrong or out of sequence, or misinterpret what happened. He or she may seem to be afraid that the event is going to happen in the future instead of having already happened. They may seem to be constantly on the watch for signs of the event happening so that they can, in some way, prevent it. This is probably similar to the adult feeling that if they'd only paid more attention, a tragedy could have been avoided.

If you suspect a child may have PTSD, another thing to watch for is that they may 'act out' parts of the triggering event while they are playing. A child who has witnessed a violent attack might stage such an attack with their soft toys, having Bunny beat up Teddy, or else get their friends to act out a play repeat of the event. It's easy for adults to misinterpret this as aggression in the child while the truth is that they're probably trying to soothe their own fears about what happened by 'controlling' the event through play.

Children Aged 12-18

The symptoms of PTSD in older children reveal themselves much more like those in adults. They tend to be more aggressive, not just towards others but to themselves, as well. They may self-harm by cutting themselves, abuse drugs or alcohol, experience eating disorders and become problem students in school. They are distrustful of others, displaying feelings of inferiority, anxiety, sadness, anger and isolation. This is particularly so in children who have been sexually abused. Children with a history of sexual abuse may act out with inappropriate sexual behaviour beyond their age group.

Therapy for children with PTSD

The good news is that for many children the effects of a traumatic experience, even when symptoms of PTSD are present, last for only a few weeks or months. The bad news is that, if untreated, some children continue to experience PTSD symptoms for years, even into adulthood. Or, as we discussed earlier, a child may appear to be okay and yet a relatively minor traumatic stressor later in life may prompt complex PTSD.

Therapy for children is similar in many ways to the adult treatments, as therapists and counsellors design their approaches to individual clients.

The first step in treating a child is to determine the extent and severity of the symptoms and to assure her that her reaction is normal considering the trauma she has experienced. At this stage there will be 'emergency intervention' if needed, with referrals for specialised treatment for serious behavioural problems such as drug/alcohol dependence, self-harm, inappropriate sexual behaviour, violence or lack of impulse control, or suicidal thoughts. If necessary, social services may be called in and the child removed from an unsafe home.

Where groups of children may have been affected, such as in a serious assault or shooting at school, there are programmes designed to offer emergency support to help them understand what has happened and that their reactions are 'the normal reactions of a normal person to an abnormal event'. The professionals running these programmes teach the children how to deal with anxiety and stress feelings, and those who are identified with more severe reactions will be referred for further help.

Cognitive behavioural therapy encourages the child to talk about what happened and how he feels about it. The therapist will teach coping strategies to help with panic attacks, depression, anxiety and stress, along with self-assertion and ways to counter negative thoughts. You may be impatient if therapy seems to be going slowly, as you naturally want your child to return to their happy, confident self as quickly as possible. It's important, however, to be patient and not rush things. The child needs to be helped to come to terms with what has happened without being distressed or uncomfortable with the thoughts, feelings and memories they are working out. The therapist will also help parents to understand the effects of PTSD and to develop ways of coping with their child's behaviour and anxieties.

Play therapy is used particularly with younger children to help them to access their feelings about what has happened. Young children often lack both the experience and the vocabulary to explain how they feel verbally, so therapists encourage them to express themselves by drawing pictures, playing games, and using dolls and other toys.

What you can do to help

If you think your child, or a child you know, is suffering from PTSD, here's what you can do to help:

- First of all, get your child checked by the family doctor, or encourage parents or caregivers to do so, to ensure there's no underlying physical illness.

- Once a diagnosis of possible PTSD is reached, the child will probably be referred to a therapist who will assess their needs and provide therapy. Learn everything you can about PTSD so you can gain an understanding of what is going on with the child. Reading this book is a good start. You can find a lot of information from the Internet, as well as obtain leaflets and other recommended reading from various organisations – see the help list at the end of this book.

- Watch the child for symptoms such as anxiety or panic attacks, problems sleeping (including nightmares), angry outbursts, irritability, unexplained sudden fears of certain places or people, reluctance to go to school, or avoiding friends and activities they usually enjoy.

- Enlist the help of the child's teachers – problems at school – from discipline breaches to truancy and falling marks – can be indicators that the child is having difficulty recovering from the trauma. Explain the problem and ask teaching staff to help with the therapy.

Case study

Our daughter became increasingly moody. We thought it was a combination of leaving her friends behind to go to a new secondary school, and teenager moods. Jenny had been such a warm and sunny child, a good student and sweet and loving to her little sister, we were shocked at the changes in her but thought time would make it all better. Her teachers called about her behaviour in class and truancy, and our younger child, Emma, became very withdrawn – we found out later that she'd borne the brunt of Jenny's sudden rages and violent outbursts when the two of them were home alone after school. It wasn't until we found Jenny in the bathroom with her wrists slashed that we faced how serious it was. In therapy we discovered that a neighbour had been sexually abusing her for several years when she was younger, and then being bullied in the new school had been the last straw. Looking back, the clues were all there but we'd missed them. Jenny is starting to recover now, but it's been a long road and I'm afraid of the effect all this may have had on Emma.

Chris, mother of Jenny, PTSD survivor, and Emma.

Children are very vulnerable to bullying at school, to abuse at home, and to sexual abuse. They believe their abuser when he threatens to burn down their house, or that a parent or sibling will be killed if they tell anyone what is happening to them. Enduring this long-term stress, while keeping the terrible secret locked inside them, can be a terrible burden for a child, often resulting in 'acting out' behaviours, discipline problems, and in older children the use of alcohol and drugs.

In some children the burden is just too great and they may repress the memory to an extent that they no longer remember in later years what has happened to them. At some point a relatively minor stressful event may trigger full-blown complex PTSD and then the child has to deal not just with the recent stressor but with the past as well.

Summing Up

It is now understood that children can suffer from a variety of mental disturbances once thought to only affect adults; these include PTSD, depression and obsessive-compulsive disorder.

The symptoms in older children are very similar to those in adults, while younger children, who perhaps lack the life experience and vocabulary to describe their feelings, may act out their PTSD in different ways.

One thing to remember is that a child might find an event very frightening and stressful because of their lack of experience and understanding. Sometimes events that an adult might take in their stride may be frightening to a young child.

A child may act out their reactions to PTSD in various ways which may be initially interpreted as discipline problems or learning disabilities. Teenage PTSD symptoms may even be dismissed as typical teenage moodiness and rebellion.

If you are the parent or caregiver of a traumatised child, then you have your work cut out for you. You need first of all the courage to admit there is a problem, then you need patience and compassion to get the child the help they need and to cope with his behaviour in every day life. On top of that, you may need to cope with siblings who don't understand the child's problem, but who do want their share of your attention!

Getting your child the help they need now, however stressful it may be, will eventually alleviate the problem behaviours and perhaps save your child from facing a full-blown case of complex PTSD at some point in their adult life.

Chapter Eleven

The Families of PTSD Sufferers

The 'wounded' person isn't the only one who suffers through the PTSD experience. Spouses, partners, children, extended families, friends and colleagues all suffer to a greater or lesser degree alongside the trauma survivor. Because PTSD tends to last for a long time and, of course, there are no obvious wounds, it can be hard for other people to cope with what's happening to you.

Case study

The psychologist says that I am disabled but not crippled. It's a good way of putting it. Unfortunately, my wife expects me to be able to perform like I used to, like other people without PTSD can. We end up arguing. It makes her mad when I don't function as she expects me to, when I can't hold a job or socialise or even take care of things around the house. I'm not asking her to look after me, I'd just like her to hold onto her patience and let us work around what has happened. If I'd come home with an arm shot off or a leg missing, she'd be able to make allowances for the things I couldn't do. I know that I screw up a lot, that I don't get things done as well or as fast as she thinks I should, and that I don't relate to our kids as a good father should. I don't do these things on purpose; my memory blanks out and my thoughts start to race and I can't keep my mind straight. Then I start to panic.

Returning Afghanistan veteran.

Because PTSD is considered by many to be a weakness or a mental health issue, or even, in the military, a sign of cowardice, it's not surprising that a lot of people don't wish to own up to the symptoms. They may be afraid that they will risk their jobs or future promotions if this goes on their personnel file. They refuse to seek treatment even though their PTSD symptoms may be frightening and intrusive, and may be causing them to become dysfunctional.

Sometimes it may seem easier to simply deny the symptoms or to blame the resulting behaviour on other factors, rather than admit to being in need of help.

If someone you care about is diagnosed with PTSD

A family member, friend, work colleague or someone else that you care about has been diagnosed with PTSD. What can you do to help them cope?

Acceptance is a big thing – this is the same person he or she has always been, but right now they're trying to recover from the 'invisible wounds' left behind by a very stressful and probably life-threatening event. Be patient. If your friend wants to talk about what happened, let him. If he wants to be quiet, accept that too. He may be experiencing a sense of being overwhelmed by everything, of being unsafe and anxious.

Encourage your loved one to seek professional help and to follow through on therapy or other treatment programmes. Join them in an exercise programme, just go running or swimming together, or explore healthy diet options – these are all things that help improve a sense of wellbeing. Offer whatever support you can – help with chores, getting to work or to counselling, therapy group, and so on. The everyday routines of life can become overwhelming for someone with PTSD – help them keep up with daily life.

10 things not to say to someone with PTSD:

- It's over now, forget about it.
- Probably better not to talk about it, there's no sense dwelling on what happened.

- You're lucky – other people died, so stop complaining.

- Get on with your life.

- You're making everyone else unhappy, stop being so selfish.

- I think you're just looking for attention and making a fuss.

- It's time you grew up and put all that behind you.

- It really wasn't as bad you you're making out.

- You'd feel better if you took up a hobby, something to take your mind off the past.

- You must have been a bit weak-minded before all this happened; other people experienced the same thing and they're not carrying on like you.

Remember that unless you are a qualified professional in medicine, psychology or counselling, it's not wise for you to try to 'cure' this person. Pushing at the wrong times could even do more harm than good. Sometimes, just being there is enough.

That said, it's important that you take care of yourself, too. People with PTSD can have wild mood swings, sudden bursts of anger, depression, or self-destructive feelings. They may experience flashbacks when they believe – and even act as if – the traumatic event is occurring all over again. Sometimes they suffer frightening dreams in which they relive the whole thing. This can be quite scary for anyone witnessing it. Violent behaviour can occur, including domestic abuse. While you may love someone dearly, you should not be the target of such behaviour and should immediately either leave the vicinity or call for help from the doctor or police.

Be aware that a fairly high number of people with PTSD do self-harm or even commit suicide. Look for sudden behavioural changes – for example, such as retreating from social contact, missing work, being late, not attending treatment sessions, 'accidents', not showing up for activities you've agreed upon. Sometimes, people considering suicide will 'make peace' with people they think they've hurt – although this can also be a therapy step! – and also give away much-loved possessions. If your loved one's behavioural changes are causing you concern, contact their doctor, or call one of the hotlines and ask for advice.

The National Institute for Health and Clinical Excellence has recommended that doctors provide the following services to their PTSD patients (the organisation's website is listed at the back of this book):

- Consider and, when appropriate, assess the impact of the traumatic event on all family members and consider providing appropriate support.

- With the consent of the PTSD sufferer where appropriate, inform their family about common reactions to traumatic events, the symptoms of PTSD, and its course and treatment.

- Inform families and carers about self-help and support groups and encourage them to participate.

- Effectively coordinate the treatment of all family members if more than one family member has PTSD.

- Provide practical advice to enable people with PTSD to access appropriate information and services for the range of emotional responses that may develop.

- Identify the need for social support and advocate for the meeting of this need.

- Consider offering help and advice on how continuing threats related to the traumatic event may be alleviated or removed.

Things you can do to help

- Spend time with the person, just being there.

- Listen, if he or she wants to talk.

- Don't push if he or she doesn't want to talk.

- Let them talk, without interrupting.

- Ask questions, but know when to stop.

- Don't compete with them by reciting your own awful experiences unless there's a relevance.

- Encourage them to keep up with treatment and therapy groups.

- Encourage them to 'get back into life' when they're ready.

- Try to involve him in exercise and general social life that you once shared.
- Most importantly, watch out for any sudden changes in attitude or behaviour that might signal a crisis.

If you are in a relationship with, or a family member of, someone suffering from PTSD, you might benefit from joining a support group yourself. Ask at your local clinic, doctor's office, contact the therapist, or the organisation that runs a PTSD therapy group. You might find help in the community services directory. If there's nothing available, consider seeing a therapist yourself, just to keep yourself focused.

Case study

My dad seemed like a stranger when he came home; a frightening stranger. Once he'd enjoyed being with me and my brother, and we'd done all sorts of fun things together. But after his last tour of duty he seemed very angry all the time; sometimes he'd shout at us over nothing at all. Once I thought he was going to hit me – instead, he put his fist through the wall. He and our mum fought a lot about his behaviour, and he never wanted to go out. I know he drank a lot, too. Even though it's more peaceful around our house since he left, I love my dad and miss him a lot. Mum said he needs to see a special doctor to get his head straight. I hope he does that soon.

Petey, 11

It could be that you have purchased this book because someone close to you who has experienced a severe trauma is now showing erratic behaviours and you think they may be suffering from PTSD and you want to help. In that case, the person is lucky – in taking the information you find here and laying it out matter-of-factly, you may remove the suggestion of shame or weakness and so encourage them to accept that there is a problem and to seek help.

And that's the first step towards getting out of the jungle of terrifying and emotionally-crippling PTSD symptoms, and back to a normal, fulfilling life as a functioning member of society.

It may be important to tread lightly, though, and be aware that someone experiencing these symptoms may also be given to bouts of anger or even violence borne out of fear and frustration.

People experiencing PTSD have three times the risk of attempting suicide than people without a traumatic stress experience. They are also likely to self-medicate with drugs (both prescription and illegal) and alcohol, running the risk of getting a criminal record. The ongoing dysfunction of untreated PTSD is a deadly spiral that can lead to family break-ups, domestic violence, unemployment, alcoholism, drug addiction, criminal or violent behaviour, homelessness and an early death through ill health or suicide.

Marital and family problems

When one partner is undergoing the problems caused by PTSD, it's no small wonder that marriages and partnerships get into trouble. The stress of trying to hold things together can leave the non-PTSD spouse exhausted and stressed and possibly facing mental health problems of her or his own as a result.

People with PTSD tend to pull away from intimacy, and don't share their thoughts and feelings with their spouse. Sexual problems are commonplace and this can cause further difficulties in the relationship.

A study of veterans with PTSD in the USA showed that they were twice as likely to get divorced, three times as likely to get divorced twice or more, and tended to have shorter relationships with 'significant others' than veterans without PTSD.

Symptoms of ongoing irritability and volatility impact all family members, as well as friends and co-workers. The emotional numbing that often accompanies PTSD, and the shying away from intimacy, creates difficulties in even the most stable marriages. Children, too, suffer from the strained atmosphere between their parents and the threat of verbal or physical violence.

The partners of people with PTSD usually have to bear a much greater share of the day-to-day running of the household, childcare, and care of the PTSD sufferer as well. They may feel under constant pressure to lessen the effects on children and others in the household.

Summing Up

PTSD, like most other mental health issues, doesn't affect just one person – it impacts on everyone around them. It impacts particularly on family members, who not only have the anguish of seeing their loved one going through the pain of PTSD, but must pick up the pieces of shattered social and family lives while perhaps also coping with reduced income and living standards.

The volatile emotions that are evident in PTSD sufferers, cause many challenges to those around them – spouses must protect themselves and their children from a partner's moodiness, sudden rages and dysfunction, while trying to maintain a reasonable semblance of a normal family life Children are often frightened and bewildered by the changes that take place in the behaviour of a parent or sibling with PTSD.

If PTSD goes untreated, it can spiral into severe mood changes, uncontrolled rages, social isolation, brushes with the police, violent outbursts, and drug and alcohol abuse. People with PTSD may become suicidal. They shut their emotions away and withdraw even from the people closest to them; sexual dysfunction places further strain on a marriage.

If you're a partner or family member of someone with PTSD, do take advantage of the help and support that is available to you. The therapist will probably ask to see you and other family members at different times and that is an opportunity to talk about your loved one's PTSD from your point of view and to ask advice. See if there's a PTSD family support group in your area and don't be either afraid or ashamed to join with others who are going through an experience similar to yours. If life at home becomes at times unbearable – and this can happen – try to schedule some time out by visiting relatives or friends for a day or two. Make sure your partner understands that this is just a visit, not the end of the marriage.

The good news is that PTSD can be cured, but it takes time and the support and patience of the people close to the PTSD survivor make a real difference. Unfortunately, it can be that the stress and strain on other family members is too great and to protect themselves, they have to end the relationship.

Chapter Twelve

Exciting New Research

There is a lot of research going on into identifying, diagnosing and alleviating PTSD. Much of the resulting drug therapies are still very much in the research stage, but hold out hope for sufferers.

A new drug under study at Northwestern University in the USA, may have halted the symptoms of PTSD in mice which have been artificially stimulated to produce 'exaggerated fear responses'. The scientists say they have identified the area of the brain connected to PTSD, and are working to find ways of ending the symptoms.

In a study at the University of Minnesota and the Minneapolois Medical Centre, researchers may have found a biological marker in the brain that will make diagnosing PTSD faster and more accurate, using magnetoencephalography (MEG). The marker appears in the brains of people suffering from the disorder, but not in the brains of people who don't.

Magnetoencephalography is a non-invasive means of measuring and recording the electrical currents produced by the brain and may also be useful in diagnosing other illnesses such as multiple sclerosis, schizophrenia, chronic alcoholism, and Alzheimer's.

Researchers report a 90% rate of success in diagnosing the participants who had PTSD from those who did not. This is the first time PTSD has been accurately diagnosed in this way and opens up the possibility of easier and more accurate diagnosis of PTSD in the future.

Looking to the future

At the time of writing, 4,000 British troops will be leaving Iraq after six years of bloody warfare. 178 British soldiers and nearly 100,000 Iraqis have died. In Afghanistan, 142 soldiers have lost their lives and the war continues. This is not the kind of warfare our fathers and grandfathers were used to – it's not pitched battles with enemies identifiable by uniform. It's suicide bombers – sometimes women and children, in civilian clothing. Snipers. IED bombs hidden on innocent-looking roadsides. The returning soldiers have been involved in this type of warfare, where there is little sense of ease or safety, and where the enemy could be anyone they meet. They've seen friends and fellow officers die or be horribly wounded. These people must return home and take up their lives in a society where most of us are unable to imagine what they've experienced.

On a social level, the need to boost available services for increasing numbers of PTSD sufferers as a result of military action, peacekeeping and natural disaster rescues should be obvious. It's certainly urgent, and one way that the public at large can help is to press their political representatives to ensure that the services are increased to meet the need.

Summing Up

The prevalence of PTSD may impact everyone in our society.

Because of its wide-ranging and sometimes quite dramatic symptoms, PTSD is a condition which should be of concern to any society which values its individual members.

One of the major reasons for this is that people suffering from PTSD may have a higher incidence of drug or alcohol dependency as they attempt to soothe their symptoms. This may also lead them into crime in order to support their addictions.

Many PTSD sufferers have difficulty holding down a regular job, and get into financial difficulties which can lead to losing homes and possessions, to homelessness and poverty.

The situations mentioned above, along with difficulties with intimacy and trust, can lead to marital break-up, family dysfunction, and contribute to the loneliness and anger that are symptomatic in PTSD. In addition, because uncontrolled or untreated PTSD can involve flashbacks and nightmares which spawn violent actions, there may be domestic violence, family break-up, and criminal charges from assaults, etc.

In addition, PTSD sufferers are more likely than the general population to have thoughts of suicide, and to act on those thoughts. Sometimes, suicide may seem the only way out of the pain, distress, sense of being out of control or under threat, and anger that are symptomatic of the condition.

People experiencing flashbacks can behave in unpredictable and sometimes violent ways as they believe they are back in the traumatic situation and must take action to save themselves. The effects of the trauma are such that a person may be unable or afraid to experience intimacy, and often there is a sense of betrayal and distrust in the wider world that leads to an inability to trust both oneself and one's friends and loved ones. There's no need to add that this can be extremely destructive of the very relationships that someone undergoing PTSD needs for support.

While there is a lot of research going on which will open up new ways of diagnosing and treating PTSD, there is a growing need in the present to provide better care more quickly, in order to limit the damage that PTSD can cause to individuals, their families, community, and society in general. It makes sense that proper, timely treatment is also more cost-effective than picking up the pieces after a PTSD sufferer decompensates.

Help List

A list of emergency numbers, support groups, information pages and professional bodies. Correct at the time of writing.

Emergency Helplines

These are numbers you can call to speak to a counsellor if you are in crisis or suicidal. Another alternative is to go to your local hospital's emergency room and explain your situation to a doctor or nurse there.

Befrienders Worldwide

International Officer, Samaritans, Upper Mill, Kingston Road, Ewell, Surrey, KT17 2AF, United Kingdom
Emergency contact: jo@samaritans.org
Now under the auspices of the Samaritans, this organisation works to prevent suicide. There are member centers in Argentina, Armenia, Australia, Barbados, Belgium, Brazil, Canada, China (Hong Kong), Cyprus, Denmark, Egypt, Estonia, France, Hungary, India, Italy, Japan, Kosovo UNMIK, Lithuania, Malaysia, Mauritius, New Zealand, Norway, Poland, Portugal, Russia, Serbia & Montenegro, Singapore, South Africa, South Korea, Sri Lanka, St. Vincent & Grenadines, Sweden, Thailand, Trinidad & Tobago, Ukraine, United Kingdom (& ROI), USA and Zimbabwe. A global listing of emergency lines by country is available at: www.befrienders.org/index.asp?PageURL=contact.php.

The Samaritans UK

General Office, The Upper Mill, Kingston Road, Ewell, KT17 2AF, UK.
Tel: 08709 00 00 32.
Website: www.samaritans.org
Email: jo@samaritans.org,
Helpline: 08457 909090

The Samaritans Ireland

4-5 Usher's Court, Usher's Quay, Dublin, 8, Ireland
Tel: 01 6710071
Website: www.samaritans.org
Email: g.phillips@samaritans.org;
Helpline: 1 850 609090
Samaritans provides a confidential support service for people who are depressed, feeling distressed or considering suicide. The service is available 24 hours a day in the UK or Ireland.

Bullying Helplines

Peach Stop the Bullying

Tel: 01582 612734

Scotland's Workplace Bullying Helpline

Tel: 0131 339 9232 (Tuesday evening 7-9pm and Saturday morning 10am-midday)

ChildLine

NSPCC, Weston House, 42 Curtain Road, London EC2A 3NH.
Website: www.childline.org.uk/Pages/default.aspx
Helpline: 0800 11 11 for children
Helpline: 0808 800 5000 for adults
ChildLine is a free helpline for children and young people in the UK to talk about problems. The service is provided by the NSPCC and in Scotland the ChildLine service is provided by Children 1st on behalf of the NSPCC. The service is confidential and young people can talk about problems including bullying, abuse, gangs, pregnancy, drugs, depression and running away from home.

National Drugs Helpline

Helpline: 0800 77 66 00
Website: www.talktofrank.com
Email: frank@talktofrank.com

A 24 hour, seven days a week, free and confidential helpline for people addicted to drugs and their families.

Northern Ireland Regional office

3rd Floor, Annsgate House, 70/74 Ann Street, Belfast, Northern Ireland, BT1 4EH
Tel: 028 9024 4039
email: info@victimsupportni.org.uk
Helpline: 0845 303 0900

Parentline Plus

520 Highgate Studios, 53-79 Highgate Road, Kentish Town, London, NW5 1TL
Tel/Helpline: 0808 800 2222
Phonetext: 0800783 6783
Email contact form available on web site.
Website: www.parentlineplus.org.uk
National charity working with and for parents. As well as the support helpline, this group offers support groups, workshops, local services and training.

Scotland National Office

15/23 Hardwell Close, Edinburgh, EH8 9RX
Telephone: 0845 603 9213
Fax: 0131 662 5400
Email: info@victimsupportsco.org.uk
Helpline: O845 6039 213

Republic of Ireland

Tel: 00 353 1 408 6118
Fax: 00 353 1 408 6125
Text: 085 1337711
E-mail: info@crimevictimshelpline.ie (email form on website)
Web site: www.crimevictimshelpline.ie
Helpline: 1 850 211 407

US Veterans National Center for PTSD

Crisis line: 1-800-273-8255
Crisis line and information source

Web site: www.ptsd.va.gov/public/pages/faq-about-ptsd.asp

Victim Supportline

Victim Support National Centre, Hallam House, 56 – 60 Hallam Street
London W1W 6JL
Tel: 020 7268 0200
Fax: 020 7268 0210
Helpline: 0845 303 0900
Supportline by mail: Hannibal House, Elephant and Castle Shopping Centre,
London, SE1 6TB
Outside office hours call Samaritans at 08457 909090
Support for victims and witnesses of crime.

Women's Aid

General inquiries: Women's Aid Federation of England, Head Office, PO BOX 391
Bristol, BS99 7WS, England
Email: helpline@womensaid.org.uk
Website: www.womensaid.org.uk/default.asp
Helpline: 0808 2000247
24 hour National Helpline on Domestic Violence, provides help and information
for women experiencing domestic violence or sexual abuse.

Youthline

YouthLine Ltd, The Lodge, Coopers Hill, Bagshot Road, Bracknell, Berkshire
RG12 7QS
Helpline: 0800 376633
Email: info@youthlineuk.com
Website: www.youthlinecounselling.co.uk
Text: 07963 779007 or if texting about bullying: 07963 779003
Provides confidential free counselling to young people in Berkshire about
bullying, drugs counselling, etc., as well as counselling for children aged 8-11
and their families.

Resources

The following is a list of resources with information about organisations helping with depression and some of its attendant problems

Alcoholism

Alcoholics Anonymous

PO Box 1, 10 Toft Green,
York, YO1 7ND
Helpline: 0845 769 7555
Website: www.alcoholics-anonymous.org.uk
A support organisation with offices throughout the world. Organises support groups and meetings for people trying to give up drinking alcohol. See the website for more information and to find a group near you.

Alcoholics Anonymous Ireland

General Service Office, Unit 2, Block C, Santry Business Park, Swords Road, Dublin 9, Ireland.
Tel: 353 1 8420700
Fax: 353 1 8420703
Email: gso@alcoholicsanonymous.ie
Website: www.alcoholicsanonymous.ie
Alcoholics Anonymous in the Republic of Ireland. 'Our primary purpose is to stay sober and help other alcoholics to achieve sobriety.' *Alcoholics Anonymous does not charge fees or have religious or political affiliations.

Al-Anon

England
61 Great Dover Street, London, SE1 4YF
Tel: 020 7403 0888 (helpline 10am to 10pm, 365 days per year)
Email: enquiries@al-anonuk.org.uk
Scotland
Al-Anon Information Centre, Mansfield Park Building,
Unit 6, 22 Mansfield Street, Partick, Glasgow G11 5QP

Tel: 0141 339 8884 (Helpline is open 10 am to 10 pm, 365 days pre year)
Eire (Republic of Ireland)
Al-Anon Information Centre, Room 5, 5 Chapel Street, Dublin 1, Eire
Tel: 01 873 2699 (Helpline from 10:30 am – 2:30 pm, Mon – Fri)
Northern Ireland
Al-Anon Information Centre, Peace House, 224 Lisburn Road, Belfast BT9 6GE
Tel: 028 9068 2368
Website: www.al-anonuk.org.uk
Aimed at the families and friends of alcoholics and people trying to give up
drinking, offering support groups and meetings.

Mental Health

Andrea Adams Trust

Hova House, 1 Hova Villas, Hove, East Sussex, BN3 3DH
Website: www.andreaadamstrust.org/
Email form on site
Helpline: 01273 704 900
A non-profit charity focused on solving problems such as bullying in the
workplace.

British National Self-Harm Network

NSHN, PO Box 7264, Nottingham, NG1 6WJ
Email: nshnca@hotmail.co.uk
Website: www.nshn.co.uk
Support for self-harmers and their families, this site also campaigns for better
understanding of this illness.

CombatStress.

Tel: 01372 587000
Email: contactus@combatstress.org.uk
Website: www.combatstress.ca
Supports discharged members of the military and merchant navy experiencing
mental health problems, including post-traumatic stress disorder with a
regional network of welfare officers available to visit at home or in hospital.

Disaster Action

No.4, 71 Upper Berkeley St, London, W1H 7DB
Telephone 01483 799 066
E-mail: pameladix@disasteraction.org.uk
Website: www.disasteraction.org.uk/post_traumatic_stress_disorder.htm
Wide range of information for survivors of disasters, people involved in rescue work, etc, and issues affecting them including PTSD.

Dublin Rape Crisis Centre site

The Dublin Rape Crisis Centre, 70, Lower Leeson Street, Dublin 2, Ireland
Freephone: 1 800 778 888
Website: www.drcc.ie
Email: rcc@indigo.ie
Provides contact details, help and resources for victims of rape and other sex crimes. Lists contact details for centres around Ireland. Has a 24 hour a day free phone hotline.

GROW

Infoline: 1890 474 474
Email: info@grow.ie
Website: www.grow.ie
An Irish support group of people who suffer or have suffered from mental illness. Local groups in many areas. GROW is a mental health organisation supporting people who have suffered, or are suffering, from mental health problems. Has a '12-step' programme.

Medical Foundation for the Care of Victims of Torture

Medical Foundation London, 111 Isledon Road, Islington, London, N7 7JW
Switchboard: 020 7697 7777
Fax: 020 7697 7799
Email: email form on website.
Asylum Team Fax: 020 7697 7799
Legal Officer Fax: 020 7697 7740
Website: www.torturecare.org.uk

Mind For Better Mental Health, England & Wales

15-19 Broadway, London E15 4BQ
020 8519 2122
Mind Cymru
3rd Floor, Quebec House
Castlebridge, 5-19 Cowbridge Road East
Cardiff, CF11 9AB
029 2039 5123
Website: www.mind.org.uk
Email: contact@mind.org.uk
Provides services throughout England & Wales for people with mental health problems, and campaigns for better treatment, patients' rights, and better medical practices.

Northern Ireland Association for Mental Health (NIAMH)

Northern Ireland Association for Mental Health, Central Office, 80 University St., Belfast, BT7 1HE
Tel: 028 9032 8474
Email: AlisonDeane@niamh.co.uk
Website: www.niamh.co.uk/
Provides local support and aims to raise awareness of mental health issues. Support services across Northern Ireland includes housing schemes, home support, advocacy and research as well as public education and information.

Northern Ireland Centre for Trauma & Transformation

2 Retreat Close, Kittyclogher Road, Omagh, Co. Tyrone, NI. BT79 0HW
Tel: 028 822 51500
Website: www.nictt.co.uk
Email: infor@nictt.org
Post-traumatic stress and related illnesses and research. The Centre provides a trauma-focused cognitive therapy treatment programme for people suffering from Post-traumatic stress disorder (PTSD) and related conditions. Subject to capacity this service is available to people affected by incidents linked to the Northern Ireland conflict (The Troubles) and other (non-Troubles) traumatic experiences.

PsychNet-UK

Website: www.psychnet-uk.com/clinical_psychology_schizophrenia1.htm
A huge online source for medical information, including a section of mental health information and Information on schizophrenia for professionals, families, and students.Online support groups and links.

Rape Crisis Federation

Rape Crisis (England & Wales) BCM Box 4444, London, WC1N 3XX
Tel: 0808 802 9999 (9am-5pm, Monday-Friday)
Email: info@rapecrisis.co.uk
Website: www.rapecrisis.co.uk
Advice and support for victims of rape and sexual assault. Co-ordinates rape crisis centres around the country, and specialist services for women and girls who have experienced rape.

Relationships Scotland

18 York Place, Edinburgh, EH1 3EP
Has an email contact form on the website: www.relationships-scotland.org.uk
Counselling, family mediation, family support. Scottish Charity formed from the merger of Relate Scotland and Family Mediation Scotland.

Relate UK

To find your nearest Relate office, telephone: 0300 100 1234
Website: www.relate.org.uk
Advice on relationship counselling, sex therapy, and has workshops, mediation consulting and face-to-face or phone counselling.

Saneline

1st Floor Cityside House, 40 Adler Street, London, E1 1EE
Tel. 020 7375 1002
Fax. 020 7375 2162
Email: info@sane.org.uk
Website: www.sane.org.uk
Helpline: 0845 767 8000
Email: sanemail@sane.org.uk

A national out of hours telephone helpline providing information and support for anyone affected by mental health problems including families and carers.

The Black Dog

www.theblackdog.net
An Irish site specifically for men which provides information on psychological health. Chatroom and discussion groups.

The Experience Project

A site offering group discussions and a chance to have your say and get advice from fellow sufferers: www.experienceproject.com/groups/Was-Misdiagnosed-With-Bipolar-But-Have-Ptsd/31934
Medical, social and psychotherapeutic help and support for victims of torture. Site has news, facts, and survivor stories as well as a treatment referral facility. Also has offices in North East & North West England & Scotland – contact details available on main website contact page.

The National Institute for Health and Clinical Excellence

Midcity Place, 71 High Holborn, London, WC1V 6NA
Tel: +44 (0) 845 003 7780
Fax: +44 (0) 845 003 7784
Email: nice@nice.org.uk
Web page for PTSD: www.nice.org.uk/search/guidancesearchresults.jsp?keywords=PTSD&searchSite=on&searchType=All&newSearch=1
Organization which developes national guidelines for the National Health Service, contains articles on treatment of PTSD

The UK National Work-Stress Network

UK National Work-Stress Network, 9 Bell Lane, Syresham, BRACKLEY, NN13 5HP
Tel: 07966196033
Email: iandraper@nasuwt.net
Website: www.workstress.net
Online tools, advice and guidance to help deal with stress and bullying in the workplace.

Drugs

Action on Addiction, Britain

67-69 Cowcross Street, London, EC1M 6PU
Tel: 020 7251 5860
Fax: 020 7251 5890
Website: www.addaction.org.uk
Information and help for people addicted to alcohol or drugs.

Narcotics Anonymous Britain

202 City Road, London EC1V 2PH
Email: ukso@ukna.org
Website: www.ukna.org
UK Helpline: 0300 999 1212
Helpline numbers for other countries available on website.
This organisation is a voluntary community of people who have a drug problem and want to get help, regardless of what drug or combination of drugs have been used, and irrespective of age, sex, religion, race, creed or class. The only requirement for membership is a desire to stop using drugs, according to the web site.

Narcotics Anonymous Ireland

PO BOX 5793, Rathmines, Dublin 6, Ireland
Website: nairleast.org/index.html
Email: info@nairleast.org
Helpline: 086 8629308
Irish branch of Narcotics Anonymous, see above.

National Drugs Helpline

Helpline: 0800 77 66 00
Website: www.talktofrank.com
Email: frank@talktofrank.com
Help for people addicted to drugs and their families

Professional Organisations

British Association of Counselling and Psychotherapists

BACP House, 15 St John's Business Park, Lutterworth, Leicestershire LE17 4HB, United Kingdom
Email: bacp@bacp.co.uk
Website: www.bacp.co.uk
Helpdesk Number: 01455 883300
Information for members of the public and health professionals, sets standards for counselling and psychotherapy, and has a training section. Has articles about various mental health topics such as self-harm, depression and relationships. Has helpdesk service to help clients find therapists.

Irish Association for Counselling & Psychotherapy (IACP)

21 Dublin Road, Bray, County Wicklow.
Tel: 00 353 1 2723427
Fax: 00 353 1 2869933
Website: www.irish-counselling.ie/index.htm
Email. iacp@iacp.ie
Referral Helpline: 01 272 34 27
Sets standards and criteria for counselling and psychotherapy in Ireland, and has a telephone referral helpline as well as information about counselling.

Oxford Cognitive Therapy Centre (OCTC)

Oxford Cognitive Therapy Centre, Warneford Hospital, Oxford, OX3 7JX
Email: octc@obmh.nhs.uk
Telephone/fax
Tel: 01865 223986
Fax: 01865 226331
Website: www.octc.co.uk
Based in the Oxford Psychology Department, part of Oxfordshire Mental Healthcare NHS Trust. This website gives information about a number of self-help booklets and informational booklets about cognitive behavioural therapy for depression, obsessive-compulsive disorder, bulimia nervosa and anorexia nervosa, anxiety disorders and others.

The British Association of Behavioural and Cognitive

Royal College of Psychiatrists

17 Belgrave Square, London SW1X 8PG
Tel: 020 7235 2351
Fax: 020 7245 1231
Website: www.rcpsych.ac.uk/mentalhealthinfo/problems/ptsd/
posttraumaticstressdisorder.aspx
A wealth of information on mental health issues including PTSD

Psychotherapies (BABCP)

Imperial House, Hornby Street, Bury, Lancashire, BL9 5BN
Website: www.babcp.com
This site has a register of qualified practitioners and provides a series of
informational pamphlets on a wide range of mental health issues from anxiety
disorders, depression, phobias, schizophrenia, eating disorders, bipolar
depression, as well as self-help information. There is a small fee for the
pamphlets.

UK Council for Psychotherapy

2nd Floor, Edward House,
2 Wakley Street, London EC1V 7LT
main switchboard: 020 7014 9955
fax: 020 7014 9977
e-mail: info@ukcp.org.uk
Website: www.psychotherapy.org.uk
This is an umbrella organisation with a register of psychotherapists and a 'Find-
a-Therapist' service. The Council also works to encourage research, improve
access to services, increase awareness of information, and examine complaints
against member organisations and therapists registered with the council.

UKtrauma.org

The UK's managed clinical network for trauma and PTSD.
Website includes a list of contact info for therapy services
Website: www.uktrauma.org.uk/

World Health Organisation

World Health Organisation, Avenue Appia 20, 1211 Geneva 27, Switzerland
Telephone: + 41 22 791 21 11
Facsimile (fax): + 41 22 791 31 11
Website: www.who.int/countries/gbr/en/
News about health, statistics, studies, research, outbreaks of disease, risk factors, and health financing.

In the USA & Canada

The American Academy of Experts in Traumatic Stress

203 Deer Road, Ronkonkoma, NY 11779
Phone: (631) 543-2217
Fax: (631) 543-6977
Website: www.aaets.org/
Email: info@aaets.org

Canadian Psychological Association

141 Laurier Avenue West, Suite 702, Ottawa, K1P 5J3
Tel: 613-237-2144
Toll free (Canada): 1-888-472-0657
Fax: 613-237-1674
E-mail: cpa@cpa.ca
Website: www.cpa.ca/

eHow

Canadian Health Website, information on PTSD
There is a contact form page on the website
Website: www.ehow.com/video_7534875_overcome-ptsd.html

EMDR International Association

5806 Mesa Drive, Suite 360, Austin, Texas 78731
Tel: 512-451-5200
Toll Free in the US & Canada: 866-451-5200

Fax: 512-451-5256
Email: info@emdria.org
An international list of practitioners can be found at the EMDR Institute
Website: www.emdr.com or the EMDR International Association:
www.emdria.com

MoreThanMedication.ca

A website which appears to be operated by the drug company Pfizer, but
which has a lot of information.http://morethanmedication.ca/en/about_mtm/

National Institute of Mental Health

A lot of information and booklets about PTSD can be obtained at:
National Institute of Mental Health
Science Writing, Press & Dissemination Branch, 6001 Executive Boulevard,
Room 8184, MSC 9663, Bethesda, MD 20892-9663
Phone: 301-443-4513 or 1-866-615-6464 toll-free TTY: 301-443-8431 or 1-866-
415-8051 toll-free
E-mail: nimhinfo@nih.gov
Website: www.nimh.nih.gov

PTSD Organisation of Canada

Contact page on website
Email: email: info@ptsdassociation.com
Website: www.ptsdassociation.com/index.php
Non-profit organisation with PTSD resources. This website was created for
those experiencing post-traumatic stress disorder and for their support system
of family, friends and fellow workers.

The Wounded Warrior Project

Website: www.woundedwarriorproject.org/
An advocacy group for wounded soldiers in the USA. Lots of articles, news
about government programmes, etc. Contact form on the website.

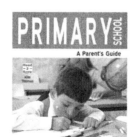

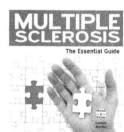

CPSIA information can be obtained at www.ICGtesting.com
Printed in the USA
LVOW03s2125050514

384571LV00003B/7/P

9 781861 441119